SURPR!SES

15 GREAT Stories with Surprise Endings

With Exercises for Comprehension & Enrichment

by Burton Goodman

Jamestown Publishers
Providence, Rhode Island

Surprises

Catalog No. 675

© 1990 by Burton Goodman

Cover and text design by Deborah Hulsey Christie
Cover illustration by Bob Eggleton
Text illustrations by Jan Naimo Jones

Printed in the United States of America

3 4 5 6 7 HS 96 95 94 93 92

ISBN 0-89061-675-2

Contents

To the Student

Surprises offers you GREAT reading. It also helps you master important reading and literature skills.

There are 15 GREAT stories in this book. Each one has a *surprise* ending. The stories will give you hours of reading fun. And you will enjoy the exercises that follow each story.

The exercises are a GREAT way to help you improve your skills:

GETTING THE MEANING OF THE STORY

REVIEWING STORY ELEMENTS

EXAMINING VOCABULARY WORDS

ADDING WORDS TO A PASSAGE

THINKING ABOUT THE STORY

GETTING THE MEANING OF THE STORY helps you improve your reading skills.

REVIEWING STORY ELEMENTS helps you understand the important elements of literature. On page 7 you will find the meanings of ten important terms. If you wish, look back at those meanings when you answer the questions in this part.

EXAMINING VOCABULARY WORDS helps you strengthen your vocabulary skills. Often, you can figure out the meaning of a new word by using clues in the context of the story. Those clues are the words and phrases around the new word. The vocabulary words in the story are printed in **boldface.** If you wish, look back at the bold words in the story before you answer the questions in this part.

ADDING WORDS TO A PASSAGE helps you strengthen your reading *and* your vocabulary skills through the use of fill-in, or cloze, exercises.

THINKING ABOUT THE STORY helps you sharpen your critical thinking skills. You will *reason* by using story clues, making inferences (figuring things out), and drawing conclusions.

Another section, **Thinking More about the Story,** gives you a chance to think, talk, and write about the story.

Here is the way to do the exercises:
- There are four questions for each of the GREAT exercises above.
- Do all the exercises.
- Check your answers with your teacher.
- Use the scoring chart at the end of each exercise to figure out your score for that exercise. Give yourself 5 points for each correct answer. (Since there are four questions, you can get up to 20 points for each exercise.)
- Use the GREAT scoring chart at the end of each group of exercises to figure your total score. A perfect score for the five exercises would equal 100 points.
- Keep track of how well you do by writing in your Total Score on the Progress Chart on page 140. Then write your score on the Progress Graph on page 141 to plot your progress.

We know that you will enjoy the stories in this book. And the exercises that follow the stories offer a GREAT way to help you master some very important skills.

Now . . . get ready for some *Surprises*.

Burton Goodman

The Short Story—
10 Important Literary Terms

Characterization: how a writer shows what a character is like. The way a character acts, speaks, thinks, and looks *characterizes* that person.

Conflict: a fight or a difference of opinion between characters.

Dialogue: the words that a character says; the speech between characters.

Main Character: the person the story is mostly about.

Mood: the feeling that the writer creates. For example, the *mood* of a story might be sad or happy.

Plot: the outline, or order, of events in a story.

Purpose: the reason the author wrote the story. For example, the author's *purpose* might be to amuse the reader.

Setting: where and when the story takes place; the time and place of the action in a story.

Style: the special way that a writer uses language. How a writer arranges words and sentences helps to create that writer's *style*.

Theme: the main idea of the story.

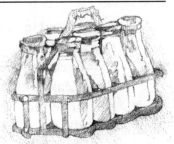

1

A Secret for Two

by Quentin Reynolds

Montreal is a very large city. But, like all large cities, it has some very small streets. It has streets like Prince Edward Street, which is only four blocks long. No one knew Prince Edward Street as well as Pierre Dupin did. Pierre had been delivering milk to the families on the street for the past thirty years.

During the last fifteen years, the horse which drew the milk wagon used by Pierre was a large white horse. The horse was named Joseph. In Montreal, especially that part which is very French, animals, like children, are often given the names of saints. When the big white horse first came to the Provincale Milk Company, he didn't have a name. They told Pierre that he could use the white horse. Pierre stroked the horse's neck. He looked into the eyes of the horse.

"This is a kind horse. This is a gentle and a faithful horse," Pierre said. "I can see a beautiful spirit shining out of the eyes of this horse. I will name him after good St. Joseph. He was also kind and gentle and faithful. He, too, had a beautiful spirit."

In less than a year, Joseph knew the milk route as well as Pierre did.

Pierre used to boast that he didn't even need the reins. He said that he never touched them.

Each morning, at five o'clock, Pierre arrived at the stables of the Provincale Milk Company. The wagon would be loaded, and Joseph would be hitched to it. Pierre would call, *"Bon jour, vieil ami* (Good morning, old friend),"* as he climbed into his seat. When he heard these words, Joseph would turn his head. And the other drivers would grin and say that the horse was smiling at Pierre.

Then Jacques, the foreman, would say, "All right, Pierre, go on." Pierre would call softly to Joseph, *"Avance, mon ami* (Go ahead, my friend)."* And this splendid team would march proudly down the street.

Without any direction from Pierre, the wagon would roll three blocks down St. Catherine Street. Then it would turn right two blocks along Roslyn Avenue. Then it went left, for that was Prince Edward Street.

The horse would stop at the first house. It would allow Pierre thirty seconds or so to get down from his seat and put a bottle of milk at the front door. Then it would go on, skipping two houses and stopping at the third. It went this way down the length of the street. Then Joseph, still without any direction from Pierre, would turn around. He would come back along the other side. Yes, Joseph was a smart horse.

At the stable, Pierre would boast of Joseph's skill. "I never touch the reins," said Pierre. "Joseph knows just where to stop. Why, a blind man could handle my route with Joseph pulling the wagon." It went on this way for years—always the same.

Pierre and Joseph both grew older together. But they grew old gradually, not suddenly. Pierre's huge walrus mustache was pure white now. And Joseph didn't lift his knees so high, or raise his head quite as much.

Jacques, the foreman, never noticed that they were both getting old. Then, one morning, Pierre appeared carrying a heavy walking stick.

"Hey, Pierre," Jacques laughed. "Maybe you got the gout, eh?"

"That's possible," Pierre said, a bit uncertainly. "One grows old. One's legs get tired."

"You should teach that horse to carry the milk to the front door for you," Jacques told him. "He does everything else."

Pierre knew every one of the forty families he served on Prince Edward Street. The cooks knew that Pierre could not read or write. Therefore, they didn't follow the usual custom of leaving a note in an empty bottle if an extra quart of milk was needed. Instead, when they heard the rumble of his wagon wheels, they would shout out, "Bring an extra quart this morning, Pierre."

"So you're having company for dinner tonight," he would call back merrily.

Pierre had a remarkable memory. When he returned to the stable he'd always remember to tell Jacques, "The Paquins took an extra quart of milk this morning. The Lemoines bought a pint of cream."

Jacques would note these things in a little book he always carried. Most of the drivers had to make out the weekly bills and collect the money. But since Jacques liked Pierre, he excused him from this task. All Pierre had to do was arrive at five in the morning. Then he would walk to his wagon,

11

which was always in the same spot at the curb, and deliver his milk. He always returned about two hours later. He would get down stiffly from his seat. Then he would cheerfully call, *"Au'voir* (Good-bye)," to Jacques, and then limp slowly down the street.

One morning, the president of the Provincale Milk Company came to **inspect** the early morning deliveries. Jacques pointed Pierre out to him. "Watch how he talks to that horse," Jacques told the president. "See how the horse listens and how he turns his head toward Pierre. See the look in that horse's eyes. You know, I think those two share a secret. I have often noticed it. It is as though they both sometimes chuckle at us as they go off on their route. Pierre is a good man, but he is getting old. Would it be too bold of me to suggest that he be allowed to **retire?** Perhaps he might be given a small **pension** to live on."

"But of course," the president laughed. "I know his record. He has been on this route now for thirty years. Never has there been even one **complaint.** Tell him it is time he rested. His salary will go on just the same."

But Pierre refused to retire. He was very upset at the thought of not driving Joseph every day. "We are two old men," he said to Jacques. "Let us wear out together. When Joseph is ready to retire—then I, too, will quit."

Jacques was a kind man. He understood. There was something about Pierre and Joseph which made people smile tenderly. It was as though each drew some hidden strength from the other. When Pierre was sitting in his seat, and when Joseph was hitched to the wagon, neither seemed old. But when they finished their work, then Pierre would limp slowly down the street. Then he seemed very old indeed. And the horse's head would drop and he would walk very wearily to his stall.

Then one morning, when Pierre arrived, Jacques had terrible news for him. It was a cold, dark morning and the air was like ice. The snow which had fallen during the night glistened like a million diamonds.

Jacques said, "Pierre, your horse, Joseph, did not wake up this morning. He was very old, Pierre. He was twenty-five. That is like being seventy-five for a man."

"Yes," Pierre said slowly. "Yes. I am seventy-five. And I cannot see Joseph again."

"Of course you can," Jacques said softly. "He is over in his stall. He looks very peaceful. Go over and see him."

Pierre took one step forward. Then he turned. "No . . . no . . . you don't understand, Jacques."

Jacques patted him on the shoulder. "We'll find another horse just as good as Joseph. Why, in a month you'll teach him to know your route as well as Joseph did. We'll. . . ."

The look in Pierre's eyes stopped Jacques. For years Pierre had worn a heavy cap. The peak of it came low over his eyes. It kept the bitter morning wind out of them. Now Jacques looked into Pierre's eyes, and he saw something which startled him. He saw a dead, lifeless look in them. The eyes were mirroring the grief that was in Pierre's heart and soul. It was as though his heart and soul had died.

"Take today off, Pierre," Jacques said. But Pierre was already hobbling off down the street. Had you been near, you would have seen tears streaming down his cheeks. You would have heard soft sobs.

Pierre walked to the corner and stepped into the street. There was a warning yell from the driver of a huge truck that was coming fast. There was a scream of brakes. But Pierre apparently heard neither.

Five minutes later an ambulance driver said, "He's dead. Was killed instantly."

Jacques and several of the milk-wagon drivers had arrived. They looked down at the still figure.

"I couldn't help it," said the driver of the truck. "He walked right into my truck. He never saw it, I guess. Why, he walked into it as though he were blind."

The ambulance driver bent down and looked closely at Pierre. "Blind?" said the driver. "Of course the man was blind. This man has been blind for five years." He turned to Jacques. "You say he worked for you? Didn't you know he was blind?"

"No . . . no . . ." Jacques said softly. "None of us knew. Only one knew—a friend of his named Joseph. It was a secret, I think, just between those two."

GETTING THE MEANING OF THE STORY.
Complete each of the following sentences by putting an *x* in the box next to the correct answer. Each sentence helps you get the meaning of the story.

1. For thirty years, Pierre had been
   - ☐ a. looking for a new job.
   - ☒ b. delivering milk on Prince Edward Street.
   - ☐ c. writing letters to the president of his company.

2. At the stable, Pierre used to boast about
   - ☒ a. Joseph's skill.
   - ☐ b. his large salary.
   - ☐ c. the wonderful job he was doing.

3. Pierre said that he would stop working when
   - ☐ a. he had saved enough money.
   - ☐ b. he was feeling too sick to go on.
   - ☒ c. Joseph was ready to quit.

4. The driver of the truck stated that
   - ☐ a. he never saw Pierre.
   - ☒ b. Pierre walked right into the truck.
   - ☐ c. the truck did not have good brakes.

REVIEWING STORY ELEMENTS. Each of the following questions reviews your understanding of story elements. Put an *x* in the box next to the correct answer to each question.

1. What happened last in the *plot* of the story?
   - ☐ a. Pierre gave the large white horse its name.
   - ☐ b. Jacques told Pierre that Joseph had died.
   - ☒ c. The ambulance driver said that Pierre was blind.

2. Which sentence best *characterizes* Joseph?
   - ☒ a. He was faithful and gentle and very intelligent.
   - ☐ b. He was stubborn and always had to have his own way.
   - ☐ c. He was not very smart.

3. What is the *setting* of the story?
   - ☐ a. a small town
   - ☒ b. a large city
   - ☐ c. the country

4. Which sentence best tells the *theme* of the story?
   - ☒ a. Two old friends work as a team and share a secret.
   - ☐ b. A horse learns a milk route in less than a year.
   - ☐ c. One should always be careful when crossing a street.

☐ × 5 = ☐

NUMBER CORRECT   YOUR SCORE

☐ × 5 = ☐

NUMBER CORRECT   YOUR SCORE

EXAMINING VOCABULARY WORDS. Answer the following vocabulary questions by putting an *x* in the box next to the correct answer. The vocabulary words are printed in **boldface** in the story. If you wish, look back at the words before you answer the questions.

1. One day, the president of the milk company came to inspect the early morning deliveries. What is the meaning of the word *inspect?*
   - ☒ a. look at closely
   - ☐ b. buy for much money
   - ☐ c. stop at once

2. In thirty years, no one had ever made a complaint about Pierre. When you make a *complaint,* you
   - ☐ a. pay a bill.
   - ☐ b. buy a present.
   - ☒ c. find fault.

3. Although Pierre was growing old, he did not wish to retire. As used in this sentence, the word *retire* means
   - ☐ a. go to bed.
   - ☐ b. go back or return.
   - ☒ c. give up a job.

4. The president of the company offered Pierre a pension to live on. What is a *pension?*
   - ☐ a. a very large house
   - ☒ b. a sum of money paid regularly
   - ☐ c. a gold watch

☐ × 5 = ☐	
NUMBER CORRECT	YOUR SCORE

ADDING WORDS TO A PASSAGE. Complete the following paragraph by filling in each blank with one of the words listed in the box below. Each of the words appears in the story. Since there are five words and four blanks, one word in the group will not be used.

The largest _city_ in Canada is Montreal. Montreal takes its _name_ from a mountain which rises in the center of the city. In 1535 Jacques Cartier, a _French_ explorer, called this mountain *Mont Réal* (Mount Royal). If you _say_ *Mont Réal* quickly, it becomes "Montreal."

> **name   city**
>
> **say**
>
> **milk   French**

☐ × 5 = ☐	
NUMBER CORRECT	YOUR SCORE

THINKING ABOUT THE STORY. Each of the following questions will help you to think critically about the selection. Put an *x* in the box next to the correct answer.

1. We may infer (figure out) that Pierre and Jacques
   - ☒ a. cared very much about each other.
   - ☐ b. didn't really like each other.
   - ☐ c. got tired of working together for so long.

2. It was hard to tell that Pierre was blind because he
   - ☐ a. always walked very quickly.
   - ☐ b. always wrote the day's orders in a little book.
   - ☒ c. kept the peak of his cap pulled down over his eyes.

3. Which statement is probably true?
   - ☐ a. Pierre was not very proud of Joseph.
   - ☒ b. After Joseph died, Pierre no longer cared about living.
   - ☐ c. Pierre was sure he could find another horse as good as Joseph.

4. Probably, Pierre didn't hear the truck coming because
   - ☒ a. he was still thinking about Joseph.
   - ☐ b. he had been deaf for many years.
   - ☐ c. he was wondering if he would lose his job.

<table>
<tr><td></td><td>× 5 =</td><td></td></tr>
<tr><td>NUMBER
CORRECT</td><td></td><td>YOUR
SCORE</td></tr>
</table>

Thinking More about the Story. Your teacher might want you to write your answers.

- "A Secret for Two" is a story of friendship and love. Explain why you think this is true.
- When Jacques looked into Pierre's eyes, he saw a dead, lifeless look in them. Why were Pierre's eyes dead and lifeless? Give at least two reasons.
- At the beginning of "A Secret for Two," Pierre said, "Why, a blind man could handle my route with Joseph pulling the wagon." Explain why this statement is important to the story.

Use the boxes below to total your scores for the exercises.

☐ GETTING THE MEANING OF THE STORY
+
☐ REVIEWING STORY ELEMENTS
+
☐ EXAMINING VOCABULARY WORDS
+
☐ ADDING WORDS TO A PASSAGE
+
☐ THINKING ABOUT THE STORY
▼
☐ **Score Total:** Story 1

17

2

The Romance of a Busy Broker

by O. Henry

Steven Pitcher was a clerk. He worked at the busy office of Harvey Maxwell, the stockbroker. Steven kept to himself at work. He always minded his own business. He almost never let any of his feelings show on his face.

But this morning Steven looked surprised. His employer, Mr. Maxwell, had entered the office at 9:30 sharp. He always did this. But today, the young lady who was his secretary arrived at the same time. She was at his side.

"Good morning, Pitcher," Mr. Maxwell said. Then Maxwell went straight to his desk. He quickly began to look through the large pile of letters and telegrams there.

The young lady had been Mr. Maxwell's secretary for a year. She was very pretty in a special way. And on this morning, she seemed to shine with happiness. Her eyes were bright. Her expression was joyful.

Steven Pitcher noticed a difference in the way she acted this morning. She did not go straight into the next room where her desk was. Instead, she waited in the main office. Once she even walked over to Maxwell's desk. She was near enough for him to be aware of her presence.

The person sitting at that desk was thinking of nothing but his work. He was a very busy broker. And he was completely caught up in his business.

Suddenly, Maxwell looked up. "Well, what is it?" he asked sharply. "Is it anything important?" His opened mail was still lying about on his crowded desk. His gray eyes flashed upon her impatiently. "Well, what is it?" he repeated.

"Nothing," answered the secretary. She moved away with a little smile.

"Mr. Pitcher," she said to the clerk. "Did Mr. Maxwell say anything yesterday about hiring another secretary?"

"He did," answered Pitcher. "He told me to go about hiring another one. I called the agency yesterday afternoon. I asked them to have a few candidates come over this morning. It's 9:45. But no one has showed up yet."

"I will do the work as usual then," said the young woman. "I'll stay here until someone comes to take my place." And she went to her desk and began to work.

Perhaps you have never been in a broker's office during the mad rush of business. If so, you may have trouble imagining it. Every minute—no, every second—is packed with work.

And this day was an especially busy one for Maxwell. The ticker began to reel out pages of tape. The desk telephone never stopped ringing. People began to rush into the office. They kept calling things out excitedly. Messengers ran in and out with telegrams and messages. The clerks in the office jumped about like sailors during a storm.

Maxwell shoved his chair back against the wall. He **conducted** business like a tap dancer. He jumped from ticker to phone, from desk to door. You would not have believed how **briskly** he did all this.

Suddenly the stockbroker realized that two people were standing near his desk. One was a young man. He had never seen him before. The other person was Pitcher.

"Excuse me," said Pitcher. "There's someone here to see you about the job."

Maxwell turned partly around. His hands were filled with papers.

"Job? What job?" he asked with a frown.

"The job of secretary," said Pitcher. "You told me yesterday to call the agency. You asked me to have them send someone over this morning."

"Are you losing your mind, Pitcher?" said Maxwell. "Why should I have given you any such **instructions?** Miss Leslie has done wonderful work during the year she has been here. The job is hers for as long as she chooses to keep it."

Maxwell turned to the young man. "There's no place open here, I'm afraid," said Maxwell. "I am very, very sorry."

Maxwell turned back to Pitcher. "Call up the agency, Pitcher," he said. "Tell them not to send any other people here."

The young man left the office. And Pitcher thought to himself that Mr. Maxwell seemed to be forgetting more and more things as the days went by.

The rush of business grew faster and faster. Orders to buy and sell were coming and going as swiftly as the flight of birds. There was no time to stop for even a moment.

At noon, finally, there was a bit of a **lull** in business.

Maxwell stood near his desk. Telegrams and messages were in his hands. A pen was stuck over his right ear. His hair hung down over his forehead. The window in his office was open because it was Spring. And today was a beautiful, a gloriously beautiful, day.

And through the window came the trace of a scent. It was the sweet scent of lilac. Mr. Maxwell stopped dead in his tracks. Suddenly, he thought about his secretary, Miss Leslie. For she wore lilac perfume.

The world of business suddenly began to fade. She was in the next room. She was only twenty steps away.

"By George, I'll do it now," said Maxwell, half aloud. "I'll ask her now. I'm surprised I didn't do it long ago."

He dashed into the other office. He rushed to the desk. He was still clutching papers in both hands. The pen was still stuck above his ear.

"Miss Leslie," he began, hurriedly. "I have only a moment to spare. I want to say something in that moment. Will you be my wife? I haven't had time to ask you in the usual way. But I really do love you. Tell me quickly, please."

"Oh, what are you talking about?" exclaimed the young woman. She rose to her feet. She stared at him with eyes open wide.

"Don't you understand?" said Maxwell. "I want you to marry me. I love you, Miss Leslie. I wanted to tell you. And I took a moment when things slowed up a bit. They're calling me to come to the phone now."

He turned and shouted, "Tell them to wait a minute, Pitcher."

Then he turned back and said, "Won't you marry me, Miss Leslie?"

The secretary acted very strangely. At first she seemed amazed. Then tears came to her eyes. She smiled through them, and slid one of her arms tenderly about the broker's neck.

"I understand now," she said, softly. "It's this business. It has driven everything else out of your head for the moment. I was shaken up at first. Don't you remember, Harvey? We were married last night at eight o'clock in the little church around the corner."

GETTING THE MEANING OF THE STORY.
Complete each of the following sentences
by putting an *x* in the box next to the
correct answer. Each sentence helps you
get the meaning of the story.

1. Miss Leslie had been Mr. Maxwell's
   secretary for
   - ☑ a. a year.
   - ☐ b. five years.
   - ☐ c. ten years.

2. The sweet scent of lilac reminded
   Mr. Maxwell
   - ☐ a. of his garden.
   - ☑ b. of Miss Leslie.
   - ☐ c. that he planned to buy some
     perfume.

3. Miss Leslie said that she would
   - ☑ a. work until someone came to take
     her place.
   - ☐ b. quit unless she got a large raise
     in salary.
   - ☐ c. never marry Harvey Maxwell.

4. Mr. Maxwell told Miss Leslie that he
   loved her when
   - ☐ a. she arrived at work at 9:30.
   - ☐ b. she said she was going to look
     for another job.
   - ☑ c. things slowed up a bit at work.

REVIEWING STORY ELEMENTS. Each of
the following questions reviews your
understanding of story elements. Put an
x in the box next to the correct answer
to each question.

1. What happened last in the *plot* of
   the story?
   - ☐ a. Mr. Maxwell told the young man
     that there was no job for him
     there.
   - ☐ b. Mr. Maxwell asked Miss Leslie
     to marry him.
   - ☑ c. Miss Leslie said that she and
     Harvey were married last night.

2. Which sentence best *characterizes*
   Harvey Maxwell?
   - ☐ a. He was very lazy.
   - ☑ b. He was very busy.
   - ☐ c. He always arrived late for work.

3. Where is this story *set?*
   - ☐ a. at Harvey Maxwell's home
   - ☐ b. in Miss Leslie's apartment
   - ☑ c. in an office

4. What was O. Henry's *purpose* in writing
   this story?
   - ☑ a. to amuse the reader
   - ☐ b. to teach the reader all about the
     business world
   - ☐ c. to prove that wealth is more
     important than love

	× 5 =	
NUMBER CORRECT		YOUR SCORE

	× 5 =	
NUMBER CORRECT		YOUR SCORE

EXAMINING VOCABULARY WORDS. Answer the following vocabulary questions by putting an *x* in the box next to the correct answer. The vocabulary words are printed in **boldface** in the story. If you wish, look back at the words before you answer the questions.

1. Mr. Maxwell jumped back and forth as briskly as a tap dancer. What is the meaning of the word *briskly?*
   - ☐ a. slowly
   - ☒ b. quickly
   - ☐ c. carelessly

2. Maxwell gave Mr. Pitcher instructions to hire a new secretary. As used in this sentence, the word *instructions* means
   - ☐ a. a great deal of cash.
   - ☐ b. some food.
   - ☒ c. orders.

3. It was very busy all morning, but at noon there was finally a lull. As used in this sentence, the word *lull* means a
   - ☒ a. quiet time.
   - ☐ b. loud noise.
   - ☐ c. difficult job to do.

4. He conducted business by dashing from the phone to the desk to the door. The word *conducted* means
   - ☒ a. carried on or directed.
   - ☐ b. rested or stopped.
   - ☐ c. left for home.

☐ × 5 = ☐

NUMBER CORRECT   YOUR SCORE

ADDING WORDS TO A PASSAGE. Complete the following paragraph by filling in each blank with one of the words listed in the box below. Each of the words appears in the story. Since there are five words and four blanks, one word in the group will not be used.

O. Henry's real name was William Sidney Porter. As a young man, Porter was accused of stealing money from the bank where he ___worked___ . It is not clear if Porter ___really___ stole the money. But ___instead___ of standing trial, he left the country. Later, Porter was ___caught___ and sent to prison. He took the name, O. Henry, from the name of a prison guard.

caught	business
worked	
instead	**really**

☐ × 5 = ☐

NUMBER CORRECT   YOUR SCORE

THINKING ABOUT THE STORY. Each of the following questions will help you to think critically about the selection. Put an *x* in the box next to the correct answer.

1. Why was Miss Leslie amazed when Mr. Maxwell asked her to be his wife?
   - ☐ a. She thought he didn't like her.
   - ☐ b. She had already said no many times.
   - ☒ c. They were already married.

2. Which statement is true?
   - ☒ a. Steven Pitcher didn't know that Mr. Maxwell and Miss Leslie were married.
   - ☐ b. Miss Leslie had been doing a poor job at work.
   - ☐ c. Mr. Maxwell didn't take his job seriously.

3. We may infer (figure out) that Mr. Maxwell asked Miss Leslie to marry him
   - ☐ a. only one time.
   - ☒ b. at least two times.
   - ☐ c. while they were having lunch together at work.

4. At the end of the story, Mr. Maxwell probably felt
   - ☐ a. sad.
   - ☐ b. smart.
   - ☒ c. surprised.

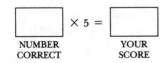

NUMBER CORRECT   × 5 =   YOUR SCORE

Thinking More about the Story. Your teacher might want you to write your answers.

- Why wasn't Miss Leslie angry with Harvey for forgetting they were married? Explain.
- Mr. Maxwell was very good at his work. Do you agree with this statement? Give reasons to support your answer.
- What is humorous, or funny, about "The Romance of a Busy Broker"? Point out as many things as you can.

Use the boxes below to total your scores for the exercises.

[ ] **G**ETTING THE MEANING OF THE STORY
   +
[ ] **R**EVIEWING STORY ELEMENTS
   +
[ ] **E**XAMINING VOCABULARY WORDS
   +
[ ] **A**DDING WORDS TO A PASSAGE
   +
[ ] **T**HINKING ABOUT THE STORY
   ▼
[ ] **Score Total:** Story 2

3

Mrs. Packletide's Tiger

by Saki

Mrs. Packletide decided that she must shoot a tiger. It was not that she liked hunting. No. Or that she believed India would be safer with one tiger less. No. The reason for her decision was this. Leona Bimbleton had flown from London to India. While in India, she had shot a tiger. Now she talked about nothing else.

Mrs. Packletide did not like Leona Bimbleton. In fact, she **disliked** her very much. She was jealous, *very* jealous of Leona Bimbleton. So there was just one thing to do.

Mrs. Packletide decided that *she* would fly to India. She, too, would shoot a tiger. Then she would return to London. She would throw a great party. She would invite all the newspapers. She would invite the photographers. She would also invite Leona Bimbleton. She would be sure to show off her new tiger-skin rug. She would make it the center of attention. That would show Leona Bimbleton!

And so Mrs. Packletide went about arranging it. First, she flew to India. Then she offered a thousand rupees for the opportunity to shoot a tiger. She made it clear that there must be very little risk involved. And she hoped she would not have to use much effort or **exertion.**

And so it happened that a little village in India **responded.** In this village there lived an old, tame tiger. It had left the jungle years ago. Now it wandered around the village, living off the smaller animals that it could catch.

The villagers liked the idea of earning a thousand rupees. They posted young men on the borders of the village. The men were given orders to head the tiger back into the village whenever it attempted to roam away.

The villagers tried to keep the tiger happy. They left it small, cheap goats to satisfy its hunger. The biggest fear of the villagers was that the tiger would die of old age before Mrs. Packletide arrived.

Finally the great day came! They waited until night. Everything was perfect. The moon was shining brightly and there were no clouds. A large wooden platform had been built in a comfortable tree. Mrs. Packletide waited there with Miss Louisa Mebbin, whom she had paid to help her.

The villagers had tied a goat to a stake to attract the tiger. This goat had a very loud bleat. It was so loud that even the nearly deaf tiger would be able to hear it. Meanwhile, Mrs. Packletide waited with a very **accurate** rifle.

"I guess we are in some danger," said Mrs. Packletide.

"Nonsense," said Miss Mebbin. "It's a very old tiger. It couldn't jump up here even if it wanted to."

"If it's an old tiger, I think I ought to get it cheaper," said Mrs. Packletide. "A thousand rupees is a lot of money."

Suddenly, the tiger appeared. As soon as it saw the goat, the tiger dropped to the ground. It decided, it seems, to take a short nap before beginning the grand attack.

"I believe it's ill," said Mrs. Packletide.

"Hush!" said Miss Mebbin.

At that moment, the tiger began walking toward the goat.

"*Now!* Fire now!" urged Miss Mebbin, excitedly. "If the tiger doesn't touch the goat you don't have to pay for it." (The goat was extra.)

The rifle flashed out with a loud *bang*, and the great beast fell to one side and rolled over in the stillness of death.

In a moment, a crowd of excited villagers appeared on the scene. Their shouting quickly carried the happy news to the village.

It was Louisa Mebbin who pointed out that it was the *goat* that had been shot—not too badly in the leg. But no trace of a wound could be found on the tiger. Evidently, the wrong animal had been hit. The tiger, it seems, had died of heart failure caused by the loud bang of the rifle.

Mrs. Packletide was annoyed at this discovery. Anyway, she was the owner of a dead tiger. And the villagers, eager for the thousand rupees, were happy to say she had shot the beast.

Later, back in London, Mrs. Packletide threw her grand party. She faced the cameras with a light heart. She spoke to the reporters. And her tiger-skin rug was admired by all. Leona Bimbleton was so angry that she refused to look at the newspapers for weeks.

A few days after the party, Louisa Mebbin stopped in to visit Mrs. Packletide. "How amused everyone would be if they knew what *really* happened," said Miss Mebbin.

"What do you mean?" asked Mrs. Packletide quickly.

"I mean how you shot the goat and frightened the tiger to death," said Miss Mebbin, laughing.

"No one would believe it," said Mrs. Packletide, uneasily.

"Leona Bimbleton would," said Miss Mebbin.

Mrs. Packletide's face looked a little green. "You surely wouldn't tell on me?" she asked.

Miss Mebbin paused. Then she said, "I've seen a charming little cottage that I would like to buy. It's quite a bargain. Only I don't happen to have the money." She looked closely at Mrs. Packletide.

Now it was Mrs. Packletide's turn to pause.

"Perhaps I can help you out," she finally said. Then she wrote a large check.

Louisa Mebbin's cottage is admired by all her friends.

"It's amazing how Louisa can afford it," they say. "She's really wonderful."

As for Mrs. Packletide, she does no more big-game hunting. She says the extra costs are too high.

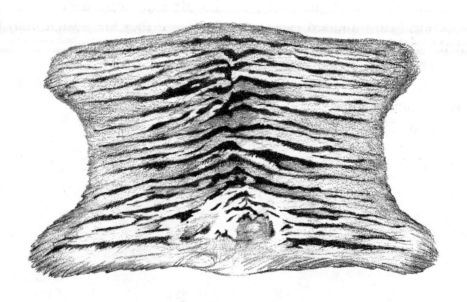

GETTING THE MEANING OF THE STORY.
Complete each of the following sentences
by putting an *x* in the box next to the
correct answer. Each sentence helps you
get the meaning of the story.

1. Mrs. Packletide went to India to
   □ a. visit some relatives.
   □ b. see interesting sights there.
   □ c. shoot a tiger.

2. After Mrs. Packletide returned from
   India, she
   □ a. threw a grand party.
   □ b. got into a fight with Leona
   Bimbleton.
   □ c. refused to speak to Louisa
   Mebbin.

3. Mrs. Packletide's tiger was
   □ a. old and tame.
   □ b. powerful and fierce.
   □ c. young and swift.

4. Mrs. Packletide gave Louisa Mebbin a
   □ a. photograph of her tiger-skin rug.
   □ b. large check.
   □ c. thousand rupees.

REVIEWING STORY ELEMENTS. Each of
the following questions reviews your
understanding of story elements. Put an
x in the box next to the correct answer
to each question.

1. What happened first in the *plot* of the
   story?
   □ a. Mrs. Packletide went to India.
   □ b. The tiger took a short nap.
   □ c. Miss Mebbin said that she wanted
   to buy a cottage.

2. Which statement best *characterizes*
   Mrs. Packletide?
   □ a. She was a very wise and loving
   person.
   □ b. She was very jealous of Leona
   Bimbleton.
   □ c. She didn't care about what other
   people thought of her.

3. Who is the *main character* in this story?
   □ a. Leona Bimbleton
   □ b. Louisa Mebbin
   □ c. Mrs. Packletide

4. Pick the sentence that best tells the
   theme of the story.
   □ a. A woman gets even with someone
   she knows—but it costs her more
   money than she thought it would.
   □ b. It is exciting to visit far-off
   countries.
   □ c. There is only one way to hunt
   a tiger.

☐ × 5 = ☐

NUMBER
CORRECT

YOUR
SCORE

☐ × 5 = ☐

NUMBER
CORRECT

YOUR
SCORE

EXAMINING VOCABULARY WORDS. Answer the following vocabulary questions by putting an *x* in the box next to the correct answer. The vocabulary words are printed in **boldface** in the story. If you wish, look back at the words before you answer the questions.

1. Mrs. Packletide disliked Leona Bimbleton and wanted to get even with her. Which of the following best defines the word *disliked?*
   - ☐ a. did not like
   - ☐ b. admired very much
   - ☐ c. enjoyed talking to

2. One village responded to Mrs. Packletide's offer of a thousand rupees. The word *responded* means
   - ☐ a. hated.
   - ☐ b. answered.
   - ☐ c. avoided.

3. Although she had a very accurate rifle, Mrs. Packletide was not able to shoot the tiger. Which group of words best defines the word *accurate?*
   - ☐ a. quiet, soft, dull
   - ☐ b. on-the-mark, exact
   - ☐ c. broken, damaged, wrecked

4. Mrs. Packletide hoped that she would not have to use much effort or exertion to shoot the tiger. What is the meaning of the word *exertion?*
   - ☐ a. pleasure or joy
   - ☐ b. discussion or talk
   - ☐ c. hard work or action

	× 5 =	
NUMBER CORRECT		YOUR SCORE

ADDING WORDS TO A PASSAGE. Complete the following paragraph by filling in each blank with one of the words listed in the box below. Each of the words appears in the story. Since there are five words and four blanks, one word in the group will not be used.

The lion has been called "the king of beasts." However, it is likely that the _____ is the more powerful
₁
animal. The tigers of _____
₂
usually eat cattle, pigs, antelope, and deer. Tigers almost always hunt at _____ . Tigers can climb
₃
_____ and are very strong
₄
swimmers.

India	night
	tiger
invite	trees

	× 5 =	
NUMBER CORRECT		YOUR SCORE

THINKING ABOUT THE STORY. Each of the following questions will help you to think critically about the selection. Put an *x* in the box next to the correct answer.

1. Which one of the following statements is true?
   ☐ a. Mrs. Packletide wanted to shoot a tiger because she enjoyed hunting.
   ☐ b. Mrs. Packletide and Leona Bimbleton were very close friends.
   ☐ c. Mrs. Packletide was afraid that Miss Mebbin would tell how the tiger really died.

2. We may infer that *rupees* are
   ☐ a. foods found in India.
   ☐ b. money used in India.
   ☐ c. small, cheap goats.

3. Why did Mrs. Packletide help Miss Mebbin buy a cottage?
   ☐ a. Mrs. Packletide felt sorry for Miss Mebbin.
   ☐ b. Mrs. Packletide owed Miss Mebbin a lot of money.
   ☐ c. Mrs. Packletide wanted to keep Miss Mebbin quiet.

4. It is fair to say that
   ☐ a. Leona Bimbleton tricked Mrs. Packletide.
   ☐ b. Mrs. Packletide tricked the villagers.
   ☐ c. Louisa Mebbin tricked Mrs. Packletide.

☐ × 5 = ☐

NUMBER CORRECT   YOUR SCORE

Thinking More about the Story. Your teacher might want you to write your answers.

- Suppose Mrs. Packletide hadn't given Louisa Mebbin a large check. What do you think Miss Mebbin would have done? Explain.
- If Mrs. Packletide had been unable to kill the tiger, one of the villagers (who was hiding) would have shot it. Do you agree with this statement? Give reasons to support your answer.
- Suppose you were a reporter at Mrs. Packletide's party. What do you think Mrs. Packletide would have told you?

Use the boxes below to total your scores for the exercises.

☐
+
GETTING THE MEANING OF THE STORY

☐
+
REVIEWING STORY ELEMENTS

☐
+
EXAMINING VOCABULARY WORDS

☐
+
ADDING WORDS TO A PASSAGE

☐
▼
THINKING ABOUT THE STORY

☐ **Score Total:** Story 3

4

The Piping-Hot Pizza Mystery

by Elizabeth VanSteenwyk

Brad hurried to Eatza Pizza. It was ten minutes past four and he was late for his after-school job. Brad liked to deliver pizzas on his skateboard and didn't want to be fired for being a few minutes late. He knew he had one of the best jobs in town.

Brad went in the back door of Eatza Pizza. "Sorry I'm late, Sam," he called to the owner.

Sam turned from the counter. He was mixing pizza dough. "Okay, Brad, but try not to let it happen again."

"Any pizzas to deliver?" Brad asked.

"Not yet, but we'll get busy pretty soon."

"Has Mr. Light called?" Brad asked.

Mr. Light was an old man who lived in a run-down house at the end of Main Street. He had called every night, Monday through Friday, since Brad had started working. Every night, he ordered the same thing—one pizza, piping hot, with everything.

Brad had been delivering a piping-hot pizza to 500 West Main Street

35

for nearly a year. Sometimes Brad wondered why Mr. Light didn't order something different from some other place. Even Brad would get tired of **devouring** pizza five nights a week for nearly a year.

Soon the telephone began to ring. People placed orders for delivery or carryout. Sam and his helper rolled pizza dough and twirled it into circles. Then they painted the circles with tomato sauce and sprinkled cheese and sausage on top. Then they placed them into the oven to bake.

At 5:15, the telephone rang. "I'll bet that's Mr. Light," Brad said.

Sam took the call, listened for a moment, then hung up and started making another pizza. "You were right, Brad," he said. "That was Mr. Light. He wants one pizza, piping hot, with everything."

"Have you ever wondered why he eats so much pizza?" Brad asked.

"Yes, I have," Sam said. "I think he's lonesome and likes to see you every day."

"That can't be it," Brad said. "He never says a word. We never **communicate.** All I see is his hand as he gives me the money and takes the pizza."

"Maybe he's too shy to talk," Sam said.

When the pizza was ready, Brad put it in a cardboard box and went outdoors. He hopped onto his skateboard. He went skimming down the street, over the **pavement**, dodging in between people. Brad really knew how to make the skateboard move, and in no time he was at 500 West Main Street. With the pizza balanced in one hand, he hopped off his skateboard. The pizza was still piping hot and smelled good. When Brad knocked at the front door, it opened right away. One old, wrinkled hand and arm reached around the door and handed Brad the money.

"Thanks a lot, Mr. Light," Brad said. "See you tomorrow." He hopped onto his skateboard and rolled down the sidewalk.

The following afternoon, Brad wasn't busy at work, so he had time to read the newspaper. The front-page headline told about the new freeway to be built on the edge of town. The story said that all the houses on the 500 block of West Main Street would be torn down.

"Look, Sam," Brad said, showing him the newspaper. "They're going to tear down Mr. Light's house."

"That's too bad," Sam said. "He'll have to move, I guess."

When Brad delivered Mr. Light's piping-hot pizza that afternoon, he said, "I'm sorry about your house being torn down. Where are you going to move?"

Mr. Light didn't say a word. He just closed the door.

Brad worried about Mr. Light for several days. When Brad delivered the pizza to him each evening, Mr. Light wouldn't talk about moving. Maybe he doesn't understand, Brad thought.

A week later, Brad read in the newspaper that the houses would be torn down the next day. When he went to Mr. Light's house that night, Brad said, "Where do you want your pizza delivered tomorrow?"

Mr. Light said nothing as he closed the door.

Maybe he has no one to help him, Brad thought. I'll come back early tomorrow morning and see if I can help him move out before the wreckers come.

Brad woke early the following morning and rode his skateboard over to 500 West Main Street. He knocked on the door, but no one answered. Then he looked in the windows, but he couldn't see anything. All the shades were down. That's funny, Brad thought. He should be up and packing.

A couple of trucks rumbled down the street and stopped in front of the house. Several workers got out and walked up to the front porch.

"What are you doing here, kid?" one of them asked Brad.

"I came to help my friend move out of his house, but I can't wake him up."

The workmen began to laugh. "Of course you can't," one of the men said. "He died about a year ago."

Brad looked at them and wondered if they were playing a joke on him. "Are you talking about Mr. Light?" he said.

"Yes," answered the man.

"He can't be dead," Brad said. "I've been delivering pizzas to him for nearly a year."

"Let's go inside and find out," one of the workers said.

"Okay," said Brad. "Let's **investigate.**"

They tried the door, but it was locked. "Get a crowbar and chop it down," one of them said. "The whole house is going to be torn down pretty soon anyway."

They chopped the door down and went inside, as Brad watched from the front porch.

"Boy, does it smell good in here," one of the workers said.

As he stood on the porch, Brad smelled something good, too. It almost smelled like . . . but it couldn't be. He climbed through the hole in the door. The workers were standing in the living room, looking puzzled.

"What's going on here?" one of them said.

Brad looked around the room. Stacked against the walls were all the pizzas he had delivered for nearly a year. They were still piping hot.

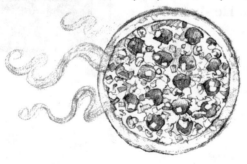

GETTING THE MEANING OF THE STORY.
Complete each of the following sentences
by putting an *x* in the box next to the
correct answer. Each sentence helps you
get the meaning of the story.

Brad delivered pizzas
- ☐ a. by car.
- ☒ b. on his skateboard.
- ☐ c. by walking or taking a bus.

. Every night, Monday through Friday,
Mr. Light
- ☐ a. stopped in at Eatza Pizza.
- ☒ b. ordered a piping-hot pizza.
- ☐ c. thanked Brad for delivering
a pizza.

. According to one of the workers,
Mr. Light
- ☐ a. moved away about a week ago.
- ☒ b. died about a year ago.
- ☐ c. really didn't like pizza.

. When Brad entered Mr. Light's room,
he found
- ☐ a. Mr. Light, asleep in a chair.
- ☐ b. cartons filled with Mr. Light's
things.
- ☒ c. stacks of pizza.

REVIEWING STORY ELEMENTS. Each of
the following questions reviews your
understanding of story elements. Put an
x in the box next to the correct answer
to each question.

1. What happened last in the *plot* of
the story?
- ☒ a. The workers chopped down
Mr. Light's door.
- ☐ b. Brad arrived late for his after-
school job.
- ☐ c. Brad read in the newspaper that
Mr. Light's house would soon be
torn down.

2. Which sentence best *characterizes*
Mr. Light?
- ☒ a. He was an old man who never
said a word to Brad.
- ☐ b. He was very friendly and said
hello to Brad every night.
- ☐ c. He was very wealthy and lived
in a fancy house.

3. Where is the beginning of the story *set?*
- ☐ a. at Brad's house
- ☐ b. at a house on Main Street
- ☒ c. at the Eatza Pizza

4. What kind of *mood* does the ending
of this story create?
- ☐ a. a sorrowful mood
- ☒ b. a mysterious mood
- ☐ c. a joyful mood

	× 5 =	
NUMBER CORRECT		YOUR SCORE

	× 5 =	
NUMBER CORRECT		YOUR SCORE

EXAMINING VOCABULARY WORDS. Answer the following vocabulary questions by putting an *x* in the box next to the correct answer. The vocabulary words are printed in **boldface** in the story. If you wish, look back at the words before you answer the questions.

1. Brad thought he would get tired of devouring pizza five nights a week. The word *devouring* means
   □ a. cutting
   ☒ b. eating
   □ c. selling

2. The workers broke down the door to investigate what was inside. Which of the following best defines (gives the meaning of) the word *investigate?*
   ☒ a. to examine or search
   □ b. to fix or repair
   □ c. to purchase or buy

3. Mr. Light never said a word to Brad, so they were not able to communicate. What is the meaning of the word *communicate?*
   □ a. see clearly
   □ b. wave good-bye
   ☒ c. exchange information

4. Brad hopped onto his skateboard and went skimming down the street, over the pavement. What is a *pavement?*
   ☒ a. the surface of a sidewalk or road
   □ b. the top of a mountain
   □ c. the waves at an ocean or lake

	× 5 =	
NUMBER CORRECT		YOUR SCORE

ADDING WORDS TO A PASSAGE. Complete the following paragraph by filling in each blank with one of the words listed in the box below. Each of the words appears in the story. Since there are five words and four blanks, one word in the group will not be used.

Although it was first made in Italy, _pizza_ is eaten today in countries
                                      1

all around the world. There are many

different kinds, or varieties, of
   2

pizza. However, just about every type of

pizza contains cheese and _tomato_
                                3

sauce. These are _placed_ on top
                     4

of a flat layer of dough which is then

baked.

---

placed	pizza
different	
tomato	**busy**

	× 5 =	
NUMBER CORRECT		YOUR SCORE

THINKING ABOUT THE STORY. Each of the following questions will help you to think critically about the selection. Put an *x* in the box next to the correct answer.

1. What was the amazing thing that took place in the story?
   - ☐ a. Brad was a few minutes late for his job.
   - ☐ b. Brad went to Mr. Light's house to help him move.
   - ☒ c. All the pizzas that Brad had delivered were still hot.

2. Which one of the following statements is true?
   - ☐ a. Brad could not ride his skateboard very well.
   - ☐ b. Mr. Light never gave Brad any money for the pizzas.
   - ☒ c. It is hard to tell whether Mr. Light was dead or alive.

3. Most people would probably consider Brad's story
   - ☐ a. very easy to believe.
   - ☒ b. quite strange.
   - ☐ c. something that happens fairly often.

4. At the end of the story, Brad probably felt
   - ☒ a. confused.
   - ☐ b. pleased.
   - ☐ c. sad.

Thinking More about the Story. Your teacher might want you to write your answers.

- This story is called "The Piping-Hot Pizza Mystery." Do you think it is a good title? Explain.
- In the story, Brad never saw Mr. Light. Why do you think the author purposely kept Mr. Light hidden from Brad?
- Suppose that Brad *had* seen Mr. Light. How do you think Mr. Light would have looked? Explain your description.

Use the boxes below to total your scores for the exercises.

☐	**G**ETTING THE MEANING OF THE STORY
+	
☐	**R**EVIEWING STORY ELEMENTS
+	
☐	**E**XAMINING VOCABULARY WORDS
+	
☐	**A**DDING WORDS TO A PASSAGE
+	
☐	**T**HINKING ABOUT THE STORY
▼	
☐	**Score Total:** Story 4

☐ × 5 = ☐

NUMBER   YOUR
CORRECT   SCORE

5

The Gift of the Magi

by O. Henry

Three times Della counted the money. It always came out the same. One dollar and eighty-seven cents. That was all. And sixty cents of it was in pennies. Pennies saved one and two at a time. Della counted the money again. One dollar and eighty-seven cents. And the next day was Christmas!

Della sat down on the **shabby** little couch. She thought about the problem. What kind of gift could she buy for Jim with just one dollar and eighty-seven cents? For several minutes Della kept **pondering** this problem.

Then Della rose from the couch. She walked to the window. She looked out at a gray cat walking on a gray fence in a gray backyard. Tomorrow would be Christmas Day. And she had only $1.87 with which to buy a present for Jim. She had been saving every penny she could for months. And this was the result. Expenses had been greater than she had figured. They always are. Only $1.87 to buy a present for Jim. Her Jim. She had spent many a happy hour planning something nice for him. Something fine and rare. Something perfect for Jim.

Suddenly Della turned away from the window. She walked to the mirror. She stood before it and looked at herself. Her eyes were shining brightly. But in less than twenty seconds, her face had lost its color. She rapidly let down her hair. She let it fall all the way down to its full length.

Now Jim and Della had two possessions in which they both took great pride. One was Jim's gold watch. It had been his father's and his grandfather's. The other was Della's beautiful hair. A queen with all her riches might have **envied** Della's hair. A king with all his treasures might have longed for Jim's gold watch.

So now Della's beautiful hair fell down about her. It rippled and shone like waves of brown water. It reached below her knees.

Then, quickly and nervously, she began to put her hair up again. She paused for a moment once. A tear came to her eyes. But she continued.

On went her old brown jacket. On went her old brown hat. With the brilliant sparkle still in her eyes, she rushed out the door and down the stairs to the street.

She stopped in front of a store. In the window was a sign. It read, "Mrs. Sofronie. Wigs Made Here."

Della caught her breath for a moment. Then she entered the store.

"May I help you?" asked Mrs. Sofronie.

"Will you buy my hair?" asked Della.

"I buy hair," said Mrs. Sofronie. "For wigs. Take off your hat and let me see what your hair looks like."

Down rippled the brown waves.

"Twenty dollars," said Mrs. Sofronie.

"I'll take it," said Della.

The next two hours went quickly by. Della spent them searching through the stores for Jim's present.

She found it at last. It surely had been made for Jim and no one else. There was no other like it in any of the stores. And she had looked through them all.

It was a watch chain—simple but beautiful. And though it was not fancy, it was very elegant. It was even worthy of Jim's gold watch. As soon as Della saw it, she knew that it must be Jim's. Twenty-one dollars they charged her for it. And she hurried home with the 87 cents.

With that chain, Jim might look at his watch in any company. The watch was grand, it was true. But, sometimes, he would just sneak a look at it. That was because he was a bit embarrassed by the old, worn leather strap that he used instead of a chain.

When Della reached home, her joy began to give way to reason. She began to fix her hair. Della did the best she could. In half an hour, her head was covered with small tiny curls. She looked at her reflection in the mirror.

"Jim will be awfully surprised," she said. "But what could I do? What could I do with a dollar and eighty-seven cents?"

At seven o'clock the coffee was made. The frying pan was on the stove ready for dinner.

Jim was never late. Della clutched the watch chain in her hand as she sat at the table. Then she heard his steps on the stairs. For a moment her hands flew to her head as she thought about her hair.

"What will he think when he sees me?" she said to herself.

The door opened. Jim stepped in and closed it. He looked thin and very serious. Poor fellow, he was only twenty-two. He needed a new overcoat and he was without gloves.

Once inside, Jim stopped suddenly. His eyes were fixed on Della. There was an expression in them that she could not read. It terrified her. It was not anger. It was not surprise. It was not horror. It was not any of the things she had been prepared for. He simply stared at her with that strange look on his face.

"Jim, darling," she said. "Don't look at me that way. I had my hair cut off. I sold it because I couldn't have lived through Christmas without giving you a present. It'll grow back again. You won't mind, will you? I just had to do it. My hair grows awfully fast. Say 'Merry Christmas!' Jim, and let's be happy. You don't know what a nice—what a beautiful gift I've got for you."

"You've cut off your hair?" asked Jim very slowly. He seemed to be having trouble accepting the fact.

"Cut it off and sold it," said Della. "Don't you like me just as well, anyhow? I'm me without my hair, aren't I?"

Jim looked around the room.

"You say your hair is gone?" he said, as though dazed.

"You needn't look for it," said Della. "It's sold I tell you—sold and gone, too. It's Christmas Eve, Jim. Don't be angry for it went for you." Della smiled, "Nobody could ever measure my love for you. Now shall I put dinner on, Jim?"

Jim seemed to awake from his daze. He gave Della a giant hug.

Then Jim took a package out of his coat pocket. He dropped it on the table.

"Don't make any mistake about me, Della," he said. "No haircut could ever make me like you any the less. But just unwrap that package. You'll see why you had me going at first."

Della's fingers tore at the strings and the paper. And then there came a scream of joy. And then, alas! a sudden change to tears.

For there lay THE COMBS—the beautiful set of hair combs she had wanted for so long. Della had seen them in a shop window on Broadway. They were beautiful combs made of the purest shell. Just the shade to wear in her beautiful vanished hair. She knew they were expensive combs. And her heart had yearned for them. But she didn't have the slightest hope of having them. And now, they were hers. But the hair she should have worn them in was gone.

Still, she hugged them to her closely. Finally, with damp eyes and a smile, she said, "My hair grows so fast, Jim."

And then Della leaped up and cried, "Oh!"

Jim had not yet seen his beautiful present. She held the chain out to him on her open palm.

"Isn't it a dandy, Jim? I hunted all over town to find it. You'll have to look at your watch a hundred times a day now. Give me your watch. I want to see how it looks on it."

But instead of obeying, Jim tumbled down on the couch. He put his hands under the back of his head.

"Della," he said. "Let's put our Christmas presents away. Let's keep them for a while. They're too nice to use right now." Jim smiled. Then he said, "I sold the watch to get the money to buy your combs."

The magi were wise men. They were wonderfully wise. They brought gifts to the Babe in the manger. They invented the art of giving Christmas presents. And here I have told you the story of Della and Jim. These two **sacrificed** for each other the greatest treasure they owned. But the gift they gave was the gift of love. Those who give with love are always the wisest. Everywhere they are always the wisest. They are the magi.

GETTING THE MEANING OF THE STORY.
Complete each of the following sentences by putting an *x* in the box next to the correct answer. Each sentence helps you get the meaning of the story.

1. Della sold her hair because she
   - ☐ a. wanted to surprise her husband.
   - ☐ b. needed money to buy a present.
   - ☐ c. didn't like the way it looked.

2. Della picked a watch chain which was
   - ☐ a. on sale.
   - ☐ b. beautiful and elegant.
   - ☐ c. so popular she saw it in several stores.

3. When Jim saw Della after she had her hair cut off, he
   - ☐ a. stared at her with a strange look on his face.
   - ☐ b. said he didn't love her any more.
   - ☐ c. said he was very disappointed.

4. Jim sold his watch
   - ☐ a. because it was old and out of style.
   - ☐ b. because he was embarrassed by the worn leather strap on it.
   - ☐ c. to get money to buy combs for Della.

REVIEWING STORY ELEMENTS. Each of the following questions reviews your understanding of story elements. Put an *x* in the box next to the correct answer to each question.

1. What happened first in the *plot* of the story?
   - ☐ a. Della went into Mrs. Sofronie's store.
   - ☐ b. Della showed Jim the watch chain she bought.
   - ☐ c. Jim asked Della to unwrap the package he brought.

2. Which sentence best *characterizes* both Della and Jim?
   - ☐ a. They were very angry because they were poor.
   - ☐ b. They both acted in a selfish way.
   - ☐ c. They cared very much about each other.

3. "The Gift of the Magi" is *set*
   - ☐ a. during the summer.
   - ☐ b. on a cold day in November.
   - ☐ c. at Christmastime.

4. Pick the statement which best tells a *theme* of the story.
   - ☐ a. You can't enjoy a gift unless it is very expensive.
   - ☐ b. The thought behind a gift is more important than the gift itself.
   - ☐ c. If you buy a present at the last moment, it will always turn out to be a mistake.

☐ × 5 = ☐

NUMBER CORRECT   YOUR SCORE

☐ × 5 = ☐

NUMBER CORRECT   YOUR SCORE

EXAMINING VOCABULARY WORDS. Answer the following vocabulary questions by putting an *x* in the box next to the correct answer. The vocabulary words are printed in **boldface** in the story. If you wish, look back at the words before you answer the questions.

1. Della sat down on the shabby little couch in their small apartment. What is the meaning of the word *shabby?*
   - ☐ a. very worn
   - ☐ b. quite large
   - ☐ c. new and expensive

2. Jim and Della sacrificed for each other the greatest treasures they owned. The word *sacrificed* means
   - ☐ a. broke into small pieces.
   - ☐ b. wondered about.
   - ☐ c. gave up.

3. A queen with all her treasures might have envied Della's beautiful hair. As used in this sentence, the word *envied* means
   - ☐ a. wanted very much.
   - ☐ b. clipped or cut off.
   - ☐ c. refused or turned down.

4. Della didn't have enough money for a gift; she spent time pondering this problem. The word *pondering* means
   - ☐ a. laughing at.
   - ☐ b. thinking over.
   - ☐ c. forgetting about.

ADDING WORDS TO A PASSAGE. Complete the following paragraph by filling in each blank with one of the words listed in the box below. Each of the words appears in the story. Since there are five words and four blanks, one word in the group will not be used.

The first watches were invented about 500 years ago. These early watches were _____ of iron and were very

1

heavy. They were really _____

2

clocks that could be carried about. Today, watches are usually _____ on

3

the wrist. In those _____ ,

4

watches were hung from a belt which was tied around the waist.

mirror	**small**
worn	
made	**days**

[ ] × 5 = [ ]

NUMBER
CORRECT

YOUR
SCORE

[ ] × 5 = [ ]

NUMBER
CORRECT

YOUR
SCORE

THINKING ABOUT THE STORY. Each of the following questions will help you to think critically about the selection. Put an *x* in the box next to the correct answer.

1. When Jim saw that Della had cut off her hair, he was
   ☐ a. pleased.
   ☐ b. frightened.
   ☐ c. amazed.

2. Which statement is true?
   ☐ a. Della found it upsetting to sell her hair, but she was willing to do it for Jim.
   ☐ b. Jim didn't really like his gold watch, so he didn't mind selling it.
   ☐ c. Della and Jim could probably have afforded to live in a bigger apartment.

3. Why did Jim suggest that they put away their presents and keep them for a while?
   ☐ a. He didn't like the watch chain and wanted to give it back later.
   ☐ b. He thought that the gifts would be worth much more later.
   ☐ c. He knew that it was not possible to use the presents right now.

4. The last paragraph of the story suggests that
   ☐ a. Jim and Della were both very foolish.
   ☐ b. the gift of love is the best gift of all.
   ☐ c. you should always give gifts that can be returned.

	× 5 =	
NUMBER CORRECT		YOUR SCORE

Thinking More about the Story. Your teacher might want you to write your answers.

- When it came to money, Jim and Della were poor. However, they were rich in other ways. Do you agree with this statement? Give reasons to support your answer.
- Della will be able to use the combs when her hair grows back. Will Jim ever be able to use the watch chain? Explain.
- According to an old saying, "It is better to give than to receive." Do you think Della believed this? Did Jim? Explain your answers.

Use the boxes below to total your scores for the exercises.

	GETTING THE MEANING OF THE STORY
+	
	REVIEWING STORY ELEMENTS
+	
	EXAMINING VOCABULARY WORDS
+	
	ADDING WORDS TO A PASSAGE
+	
	THINKING ABOUT THE STORY
▼	
	Score Total: Story 5

6

The Southpaw

by Judith Viorst

Dear Richard,

Don't invite me to your birthday party because I'm not coming. And give back the Disneyland sweatshirt <u>I said</u> you could wear. If I'm not good enough to play on your team, I'm not good enough to be friends with.

Your **former** friend,
Janet

P.S. I hope when you go to the dentist he finds 20 cavities.

Dear Janet,

Here is your stupid Disneyland sweatshirt, if that's how you're going to be. I want my comic books now—finished or not. No girl has ever played on the Mapes Street baseball team, and as long as I'm captain, no girl ever will.

Your former friend,
Richard

P.S. I hope when you go for your checkup you need a tetanus shot.

52

Dear Richard,

I'm changing my goldfish's name from Richard to Stanley. Don't count on my vote for class president next year. Just because I'm a member of the ballet club doesn't mean I'm not a terrific ballplayer.

Your former friend,
Janet

P.S. I see you lost your first game 28-0.

Dear Janet,

I'm not saving any more seats for you on the bus. For all I care you can stand the whole way to school. Why don't you just forget about baseball and learn something nice like knitting!

Your former friend,
Richard

P.S. Wait until Wednesday.

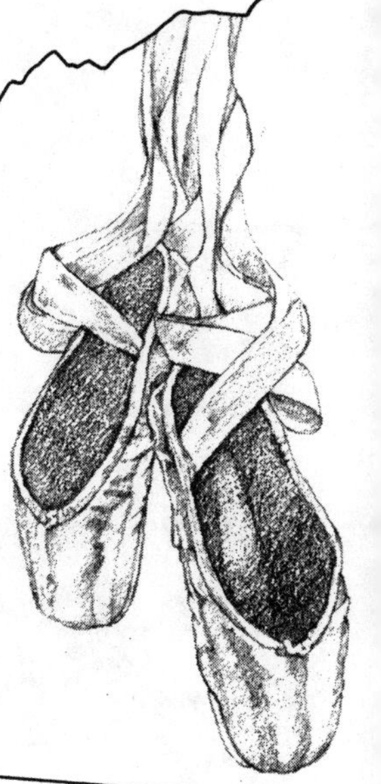

Dear Richard,

My father said I could call someone to go with us for a ride and hot-fudge sundaes. In case you didn't notice, I didn't call you.

Your former friend,
Janet

P.S. I see you lost your second game, 34-0.

Dear Janet,
Remember when I took the laces out of my blue-and-white sneakers and gave them to you? I want them back.

Your former friend,
Richard

P.S. Wait until Friday.

Dear Richard,
Congratulations on your unbroken record. Eight straight losses—wow! I understand you're the laughingstock of New Jersey.

Your former friend,
Janet

P.S. Why don't you and your team forget about baseball and learn something nice like knitting maybe?

Dear Janet,
Here's the silver horseback riding **trophy** that you gave me. I don't think I want to keep it anymore.

Your former friend,
Richard

P.S. I didn't think you'd be the kind who'd kick a man when he's down.

Dear Richard,

I wasn't kicking exactly. I was kicking back.

Your former friend,
Janet

P.S. In case you were wondering, my batting average is .345.

Dear Janet,

Alfie is having his tonsils out tomorrow. We might be able to let you catch next week.

Richard

Dear Richard,

I pitch.

Janet

Dear Janet,

Joel is moving to Kansas and Danny **sprained** his wrist. How about a **permanent** place in the outfield?

Richard

Dear Richard,

I pitch.

Janet

Dear Janet,
Ronnie caught the chicken pox and Leo broke his toe and Elwood has these stupid violin lessons. I'll give you first base, and that's my final offer.

Richard

Dear Richard,
Susan Reilly plays first base, Marilyn Jackson catches, Ethel Kahn plays center field, I pitch. It's a package deal.

Janet

P.S. Sorry about your 12-game losing streak.

Dear Janet,
Please! Not Marilyn Jackson.

Richard

Dear Richard,
Nobody ever said I was unreasonable. How about Lizzie Martindale instead?

Janet

Dear Janet,
At least could you call your goldfish Richard again?

Your friend,
Richard

GETTING THE MEANING OF THE STORY.
Complete each of the following sentences
by putting an *x* in the box next to the
correct answer. Each sentence helps you
get the meaning of the story.

1. In her first letter to Richard, Janet said
   that if she was not good enough to play
   on the team then
   ☐ a. she was not good enough to be
        friends with.
   ☐ b. she would practice and try to get
        better.
   ☐ c. it didn't make any difference to her.

2. In his first letter to Janet, Richard
   said that
   ☐ a. Janet could play anywhere she
        wanted on the team.
   ☐ b. no girl had ever played on the
        Mapes Street baseball team.
   ☐ c. he was thinking about leaving
        the team soon.

3. Because she was angry at Richard, Janet
   ☐ a. said she would never speak to
        him again.
   ☐ b. changed her goldfish's name
        from Richard to Stanley.
   ☐ c. told him to give up his job as
        captain.

4. The only way Janet was willing to play
   on the team was if she
   ☐ a. played the outfield.
   ☐ b. played first base.
   ☐ c. pitched.

☐ × 5 = ☐		
NUMBER CORRECT		YOUR SCORE

REVIEWING STORY ELEMENTS. Each of
the following questions reviews your
understanding of story elements. Put an
x in the box next to the correct answer
to each question.

1. Which statement best *characterizes* Janet?
   ☐ a. She is the kind of person who
        gives up very easily.
   ☐ b. She refused to give in when she
        felt she was right.
   ☐ c. She had no friends and very few
        interests.

2. What happened last in the *plot* of "The
   Southpaw"?
   ☐ a. Janet asked Richard to return the
        sweatshirt she said he could wear.
   ☐ b. Richard's team lost its first game
        by the score of 28–0.
   ☐ c. Janet offered Richard four
        players, all girls, for his team.

3. What is unusual about the *style* of this
   story?
   ☐ a. The story is told through an
        exchange of letters.
   ☐ b. The author uses long sentences that
        are difficult to understand.
   ☐ c. The writing is beautiful because
        the author describes nature.

4. Which word best tells the *mood* of "The
   Southpaw"?
   ☐ a. sad
   ☐ b. mysterious
   ☐ c. amusing

☐ × 5 = ☐		
NUMBER CORRECT		YOUR SCORE

EXAMINING VOCABULARY WORDS. Answer the following vocabulary questions by putting an *x* in the box next to the correct answer. The vocabulary words are printed in boldface in the story. If you wish, look back at the words before you answer the questions.

1. Danny could not play because he sprained his wrist. The word *sprained* means
   ☐ a. looked at closely.
   ☐ b. kept thinking about.
   ☐ c. hurt by a sudden twist.

2. Richard needed more players, so he offered Janet a permanent place in the outfield. Something that is *permanent*
   ☐ a. lasts for a long time.
   ☐ b. pays a lot of money.
   ☐ c. looks very good.

3. Richard returned a silver horseback riding trophy to Janet. Which of the following best defines (gives the meaning of) the word *trophy?*
   ☐ a. a birthday present
   ☐ b. a prize for winning something
   ☐ c. a ticket to a show

4. When Janet was angry at Richard, she became his former friend. As used in this sentence, the word *former* means
   ☐ a. close.
   ☐ b. past.
   ☐ c. happy.

☐	× 5 =	☐
NUMBER CORRECT		YOUR SCORE

ADDING WORDS TO A PASSAGE. Complete the following paragraph by filling in each blank with one of the words listed in the box below. Each of the words appears in the story. Since there are five words and four blanks, one word in the group will not be used.

Cy Young won more baseball games than any pitcher who ever lived. He _____ for 22 years and won 511 games. Young finally gave up _____ at the age of 44. He was still a very _____ pitcher. But he had gained so much weight, he couldn't bend down to _____ the ball.

baseball	**friends**
catch	
played	**good**

☐	× 5 =	☐
NUMBER CORRECT		YOUR SCORE

THINKING ABOUT THE STORY. Each of the following questions will help you to think critically about the selection. Put an *x* in the box next to the correct answer.

1. Clues in the story suggest that Janet was a
   - ☐ a. very poor baseball player.
   - ☐ b. fair, or average, baseball player.
   - ☐ c. very good baseball player.

2. We may infer (figure out) that Richard
   - ☐ a. finally agreed to let girls play on the team.
   - ☐ b. decided he would rather lose games than have girls on the team.
   - ☐ c. didn't care what Janet thought of him.

3. Probably, Janet wrote the first letter to Richard because
   - ☐ a. she wanted to make friends with him.
   - ☐ b. she was so angry, she didn't want to speak to him.
   - ☐ c. he asked her to write to him.

4. Which one of the following was probably the most important reason Richard changed his mind?
   - ☐ a. He wanted Janet to vote for him for class president.
   - ☐ b. He was afraid Janet wouldn't return the things he had given her.
   - ☐ c. His team had lost every one of its games.

	× 5 =	
NUMBER CORRECT		YOUR SCORE

Thinking More about the Story. Your teacher might want you to write your answers.

- Richard and Janet were good friends before the story began. They stopped being friends for a while. But they were friends again at the end of the story. Prove that these statements are true.
- Explain how Richard gave in to Janet. In what way did Janet show that she, too, was willing to give in?
- A "southpaw" is a left-handed baseball pitcher. Some people say that southpaws are known for speaking their minds. Do you think that "The Southpaw" is a good name for this story? Explain.

Use the boxes below to total your scores for the exercises.

	GETTING THE MEANING OF THE STORY
+	
	REVIEWING STORY ELEMENTS
+	
	EXAMINING VOCABULARY WORDS
+	
	ADDING WORDS TO A PASSAGE
+	
	THINKING ABOUT THE STORY
▼	
	Score Total: Story 6

7

His Father's Boots

by Charles Land

*J*ody felt the heat of the sun as it beat against his face. Now the wind was rising. He had been waiting all afternoon for his father to return.

Once more, Jody searched the distant hills. There was no sign of life. He did hear the hollow sound of a rattlesnake. They, too, were coming out of the hills in search of water. Jody had promised his mother that he would return before sundown. He headed his pony toward home.

That morning, Jody's father had left their ranch in Texas. He had gone to Grandfather's house in Mexico for help. The long **drought** had wiped out their cattle. And now the well had gone dry.

The family had been torn apart by the Civil War. Grandfather was on the side of the Confederacy. His son believed in the Union side. It was true that Jody's father had gone to Grandfather for help. But it was also a mission of peace. It was a search for kindness and for understanding. Grandfather

had said he would never forgive his son. Grandfather had said that a man who fought for the Union was no son of his.

A low golden cloud hung above the endless miles of hard, dry earth. Their white ranch house and water tank stood alone under the cloud. The windmill seemed painted against the sky.

When Jody arrived home, his mother and his older brother, Ben, were waiting at the gate. Ben was 16, nearly a man.

"Pa didn't come back," Jody said.

He looked at his mother's tired face. She tried to smile. Then she fingered her apron nervously.

"It's a good sign," she said. "He's probably staying the night. Come on, boys. Take care of your pony while I get us a bite to eat."

Their meal of chili beans and pan bread was nearly over when they heard a whinny. Jody knew it was Pa's horse. It had to be. Jody was the first to reach the front door. He was the first to see his father's lifeless body bent low over the saddle.

Ben and Jody worked together. But the dead weight was almost too much for them.

His mother sobbed. "Grandfather's shot him! That old man has shot him!"

But they found no gun wounds on the body.

Jody heard his mother's voice. The sobs were gone. Her voice was soft, but it showed strength. She put her hands on Ben's shoulders.

"You are the head of this outfit now, Ben. You will wear your father's boots. Tomorrow you will go to your grandfather. You will tell him what has happened because of this quarrel."

His father's boots! Jody suddenly felt the full force of the **tragedy.** His father's beautiful boots! They were made by one of the great boot makers of El Paso. They were his father's one splendid pride.

The boys spent hours digging their father's grave. The fresh mound needed only a cross. Jody would make one and place it there the next day.

At dawn, Jody helped Ben put on the boots. "They're a tight fit," said Jody. "Your feet are bigger than Pa's."

Ben stood up and stomped about in the boots. "I'm not afraid of Grandpa," Ben said. "I'll face him down. I don't know who killed Pa. But Grandpa's responsible. Ma says so."

"Ma can't be right, and you know it," Jody said. "Grandpa wouldn't kill his own son."

Ben stared at his brother. "You always did stick up for Grandpa!" said Ben.

Jody and Ma stood at the gate. They watched as Ben rode out across the sand. It was the longest morning of Jody's life. He made a cross from some cedar boards. The carving on the cross took the most time—Pa's name and the two dates.

Jody tried to keep Ma's mind off the quarrel. But it seemed to be all she could think about. This bitterness—the Civil War—had torn a nation apart. It could easily destroy a family. But surely Ben would be able to get Grandfather to help and to understand. Difficult as the old man sometimes was, Jody knew that Grandpa loved his grandsons.

Jody was at the corral later when he heard his mother's scream. He leaped over the fence and rushed across the sand to the house. Ma was trying to drag Ben from the saddle of his father's horse.

"He's killed him!" she cried.

But again, there were no gun wounds on the body.

"You're the man now," Ma said. "You will wear your father's boots."

Jody knew that the coming of manhood is not always determined by a boy's age. It did not matter whether the symbol was a crown or a pair of boots. He was not a man. He was not ready to wear the boots yet.

Jody pulled the boots from Ben's feet. His mother watched with grief-filled eyes. He tied the boots backward in the stirrups of his father's riderless horse.

"Have you gone mad?" said Ma. "What are you doing?"

"Grandpa will know I come in peace when he sees me leading Pa's riderless horse with his empty boots."

"It'll be your funeral, Jody! Pa's dead and buried. And Ben's dead, too. Your grandfather killed them."

"Ma, I don't believe it."

"He'll kill you, too."

Jody slowly led his mother into the house. He sat her in a high-backed rocker. The cradle-like rocking of the chair seemed to quiet her.

"Listen, Ma," said Jody, "I'm going for help. I'll be back before morning."

Jody set out into the heat. The **intense** rays of the sun shone down on him without mercy. Jody and his pony led the riderless horse across the burning sands. They traveled twenty-five miles into Mexico. Finally, Jody saw his grandfather's ranch house ahead.

63

The old man and his foreman, Juan Vargas, were sitting on the porch. When they saw the boy leading the riderless horse, they rushed out to him.

"Jody! What happened?" asked Grandfather.

Jody pointed to the riderless horse. "Father and Ben are dead."

Grandfather put his arms around the boy's shoulders. Juan Vargas followed them into the house.

"Let's get at the truth," said Grandfather. "When did it happen? Where?"

Jody told them everything. He even told of his mother's fears—of how she accused Grandfather. There were tears in the old man's eyes.

"It doesn't make sense," said Grandfather. "A strong man and a boy don't die without a cause. There must be a gun wound, or something."

"I knew you didn't kill them," Jody said.

Juan Vargas stared at the boy. "The boots, you wear them, no?"

"I'm not a man," said Jody. "When I'm a man, I'll wear them."

The foreman shook his head. "I have heard of things like this before," he said.

The old man stared into the keen black eyes of the Mexican.

"What do you think, Juan? Do you know anything about this terrible thing? I'll post a reward for the killers."

Juan Vargas got up and left the room.

A few minutes later he returned with the boots. He took a knife from his pocket. Then slowly he went over the boots with the knife, picking at the beautifully carved leather.

Jody cried out. "He's wrecking Pa's boots!"

Before Jody could stop him, Juan Vargas cut a neat patch out of the right boot. The Mexican very carefully handed the circle of leather to the old man.

"This is the murderer!" said Juan.

Buried deep in the leather was the poisonous **fang** of a rattlesnake.

GETTING THE MEANING OF THE STORY. Complete each of the following sentences by putting an *x* in the box next to the correct answer. Each sentence helps you get the meaning of the story.

1. Jody's mother thought that grandfather
   ☐ a. would be glad to see Jody.
   ☐ b. would help the family find water.
   ☐ c. had killed Pa and Ben.

2. In order to get to grandfather's house Jody had to
   ☐ a. go by stagecoach.
   ☐ b. travel twenty-five miles by pony.
   ☐ c. take a train.

3. Jody refused to wear his father's boots because
   ☐ a. they were much too small for him.
   ☐ b. he didn't like the way they looked.
   ☐ c. he was not yet a man.

4. Juan Vargas slowly went over the boots with
   ☐ a. his knife.
   ☐ b. his hands.
   ☐ c. a piece of cloth.

REVIEWING STORY ELEMENTS. Each of the following questions reviews your understanding of story elements. Put an *x* in the box next to the correct answer to each question.

1. Who is the *main character* in "His Father's Boots"?
   ☐ a. Ben
   ☐ b. Ma
   ☐ c. Jody

2. What caused the *conflict* between Pa and Grandfather?
   ☐ a. They had a quarrel over how to bring up Ben and Jody.
   ☐ b. They had a fight over money.
   ☐ c. They were on different sides in the Civil War.

3. What happened last in the *plot* of the story?
   ☐ a. Juan Vargas handed a patch of leather to the old man.
   ☐ b. Ben rode out to grandfather's ranch.
   ☐ c. Jody searched the hills for his father.

4. Where is this story *set?*
   ☐ a. in a small Southern town
   ☐ b. in Texas and Mexico
   ☐ c. in a city in the East

☐ × 5 = ☐

NUMBER CORRECT   YOUR SCORE

☐ × 5 = ☐

NUMBER CORRECT   YOUR SCORE

EXAMINING VOCABULARY WORDS. Answer the following vocabulary questions by putting an *x* in the box next to the correct answer. The vocabulary words are printed in **boldface** in the story. If you wish, look back at the words before you answer the questions.

1. The intense rays of the sun beat down on Jody without mercy. What is the meaning of the word *intense?*
   - ☐ a. very strong
   - ☐ b. very weak
   - ☐ c. very friendly

2. Jody felt that his father's death was a tragedy. As used in this sentence, the word *tragedy* means a
   - ☐ a. happy event.
   - ☐ b. terrible event.
   - ☐ c. common event.

3. The drought had wiped out their cattle. And now the well had gone dry. What is the meaning of the word *drought?*
   - ☐ a. a group of sharp rocks and stones
   - ☐ b. a long period of time without rain
   - ☐ c. a week or more of wet weather

4. Buried in the leather was the poisonous fang of a rattlesnake. A *fang* is a
   - ☐ a. thick tail.
   - ☐ b. strong smell.
   - ☐ c. long, pointed tooth.

ADDING WORDS TO A PASSAGE. Complete the following paragraph by filling in each blank with one of the words listed in the box below. Each of the words appears in the story. Since there are five words and four blanks, one word in the group will not be used.

Sometimes, rattlesnakes give a warning sound _____1_____ they strike. When a rattlesnake is frightened or surprised, it lifts its tail _____2_____ the ground. It shakes the tail _____3_____ and forth very quickly. The rattles at the tip of the tail strike against each other. That is what makes the warning _____4_____ .

off	before
	sun
sound	back

$\boxed{}$ × 5 = $\boxed{}$

NUMBER
CORRECT

YOUR
SCORE

$\boxed{}$ × 5 = $\boxed{}$

NUMBER
CORRECT

YOUR
SCORE

66

THINKING ABOUT THE STORY. Each of the following questions will help you to think critically about the selection. Put an *x* in the box next to the correct answer.

1. We may infer (figure out) that Pa and Ben were killed by
   - ☐ a. gunshot wounds.
   - ☐ b. poison from a snake.
   - ☐ c. the heat on the burning sands.

2. If he had worn his father's boots, Jody would probably have
   - ☐ a. tripped and fallen.
   - ☐ b. gotten into a fight with his grandfather.
   - ☐ c. been killed, too.

3. Clues in "His Father's Boots" suggest that the story took place
   - ☐ a. just a few years ago.
   - ☐ b. about 20 years ago.
   - ☐ c. more than 100 years ago.

4. Which statement below is true?
   - ☐ a. Pa and Ben never reached grandfather's ranch.
   - ☐ b. Juan Vargas couldn't figure out who the murderer was.
   - ☐ c. Grandfather was planning to shoot Jody.

Thinking More about the Story. Your teacher might want you to write your answers.

- Jody said that he was not ready to wear the boots yet. Do you think that he earned the right to wear the boots now? Explain your answer.
- Grandfather respected Juan Vargas—with good reason. Show that this statement is true.
- Suppose that the story continued. Do you think Grandfather would have returned home with Jody? Give reasons to support your answer.

Use the boxes below to total your scores for the exercises.

[___]
GETTING THE MEANING OF THE STORY
+
[___]
REVIEWING STORY ELEMENTS
+
[___]
EXAMINING VOCABULARY WORDS
+
[___]
ADDING WORDS TO A PASSAGE
+
[___]
THINKING ABOUT THE STORY
▼
[___]
Score Total: Story 7

[___] × 5 = [___]

NUMBER CORRECT   YOUR SCORE

8

The Angel

by Carol Chapman

*W*arren S. Fish put on his gray tie and his gray coat. He combed his gray hair and parted it neatly. Then he quietly dialed the bank's number.

"Hello, Mr. Fowler? I have a doctor's **appointment** this morning," he whispered into the phone. "I will be an hour late." Then he hung up as softly as possible.

"Warren?" came a sharp voice from the kitchen. "Warren? Who are you talking to?"

Warren took a deep breath. Then he went into the kitchen. He sat down to eat his soft-boiled egg and toast. "No one, dear," he said. "I was talking to no one."

"I heard you talking to someone, Warren," his wife said. She buttered a large jelly roll and stuffed it into her mouth. "I want to know who you were talking to!"

Warren wiped his hands with his napkin. Then he picked up his briefcase.

"Good-bye, Ethel," he said, opening the back door. "Good-bye."

As he closed the door, he could hear the sound of plastic wrapping being torn. His wife was opening another package of rolls.

69

Warren drove two blocks. Then he parked his car. It was not a **medical** building he went into. It was a travel agency.

"A one-way ticket to the Hawaiian Islands, please," he told the agent.

"What part of the Islands?" asked the agent.

"Any part. It doesn't matter. Just so I can leave tonight," explained Warren.

The travel agent made a phone call. Then she spoke to Warren.

"Sir, there is a seat for you at 8:25 for Maui. Would you like to pay now?"

"No," said Warren. "I don't have the money now. But," he smiled, "I will tonight."

"And what is your name?" she asked.

Warren thought a minute. "My name is James Strut!" he said in a deeper voice.

The agent told Warren his flight number. He thanked her in his new, deep voice. Then he drove to Greyson's Department Store. He bought shirts and pants. Not gray shirts or gray pants, but bright, flowery shirts and white pants. Then he bought some luggage.

He put everything in the trunk of his car. Then he looked at his old watch. It was now time to go to the bank. He drove to the old part of town, to the First American Bank—the bank Warren had driven to for 45 years.

"There's Warren," Mr. Fowler said, when Warren walked through the doorway.

Warren nodded at the young bank manager.

"Well, how does it feel?" said Mr. Fowler. "Your last day here. You get to retire at last."

"Yes, sir," said Warren. "I'm looking forward to it."

"Your voice sounds different," said Mr. Fowler.

Warren just smiled.

During the morning, Warren greeted his usual customers. He said the usual nice things to them. Some customers even brought in some "good-bye" gifts like small plants. They should have brought me suntan oil and sunglasses. Or maybe a beach chair, Warren thought, as he looked at the pile of gifts. In the meantime, Warren kept watching the clock. Time was going by slowly for him.

When lunchtime came, Mr. Fowler took Warren out to lunch at a fancy place. He gave Warren a gold watch.

"It's not much after 45 years," said Mr. Fowler.

"Oh, it's very nice," Warren said. He put it on. "Is it waterproof?"

"Waterproof?" asked Mr. Fowler in surprise. "Well, I guess it is."

"Good," said Warren. A waterproof watch would be a must on his new 22-foot sailboat.

"I know the small amount of money you'll be getting every month isn't very much," Mr. Fowler said, shaking his head. "But you'll get by."

"I'm sure I will," said Warren.

Warren knew he would more than get by after today. He would have plenty of money. Every week for the past 40 years, Warren had been putting away a new, crisp, $50 bill. Even though it was the bank's money, he felt he deserved it. He had found a way to change the books so the bank never missed the money. It was foolproof!

He had been working at the bank for five years. Then he discovered the loose brick close to the floor, in the wall next to his desk. When he pulled the loose brick out, there was a big, empty space. And that was where Warren had stored his money. He would have over $100,000 by now.

Ten minutes before closing time, Warren began to get very excited. He planned to make some excuse for staying a little late—like clearing out his desk. Then, when everyone was gone, he would pile the money into his briefcase. Then he would head for the airport.

"Mr. Fish!" came a woman's voice.

Warren looked up to see Mrs. Angelo. Mrs. Angelo came in every Friday to make a **deposit**. She always came to his window. Her bakery was right next door to the bank. It had been there as long as he could remember.

"I will miss you, Mr. Fish," she said. "Please take these to your wife." She handed him a white bag. He looked into it and saw five different kinds of jelly rolls.

"Why, thank you," said Warren. "I'll mail them to her."

"What do you mean?" asked Mrs. Angelo.

"I was just joking," said Warren.

He took the money from her and counted it out. She always made two deposits, one for her checking account and one for her savings.

"Mr. Fish, I will tell you a secret. I have an angel," Mrs. Angelo declared.

Warren hoped this wasn't going to take long. It was almost closing time, and sometimes she could talk forever.

"Is that right?" said Warren.

"Yes, I will tell you about it. My angel first came to me 30 years ago. I had no money to pay the rent on my bakery. I prayed and prayed, but nothing happened."

Warren looked at the clock. It was two minutes until closing time.

She went on. "So I started packing up the things in my shop. I was cleaning out a bottom cupboard. I reached in and there was the money!" Mrs. Angelo started laughing. "It was my angel, you see. My angel sent me the money."

"That's very nice," said Warren as he locked his drawer. He had things to do, and she was slowing him up!

"And ever since, my angel has given me money in that very spot every single week. I'm sending my grandchildren to college with it now!"

Suddenly Warren looked up, his voice becoming **shrill**. "Every week you say? How much does your angel give you?" Sweat started to form on his forehead.

"A brand new $50 bill," said Mrs. Angelo. "Straight from heaven!"

GETTING THE MEANING OF THE STORY.
Complete each of the following sentences
by putting an *x* in the box next to the
correct answer. Each sentence helps you
get the meaning of the story.

1. Every week, Warren Fish had been
   putting a $50 bill in
   ☒ a. a big, empty space in the wall.
   ☐ b. his bank account.
   ☐ c. his desk at home.

2. Mr. Fowler gave Warren
   ☐ a. some small plants.
   ☐ b. suntan oil and sunglasses.
   ☒ c. a gold watch.

3. Mrs. Angelo said that she had been
   receiving money from
   ☐ a. Mr. Fish.
   ☒ b. an angel.
   ☐ c. sales at the bakery.

4. Warren thought that he
   ☐ a. would miss working at the bank.
   ☐ b. should really return the money
       he had taken.
   ☒ c. had put more than $100,000
       aside.

<table>
<tr><td>☐</td><td>× 5 =</td><td>☐</td></tr>
<tr><td>NUMBER
CORRECT</td><td></td><td>YOUR
SCORE</td></tr>
</table>

REVIEWING STORY ELEMENTS. Each of
the following questions reviews your
understanding of story elements. Put an
x in the box next to the correct answer
to each question.

1. What happened last in the *plot* of
   the story?
   ☐ a. Mr. Fowler took Warren out to
       lunch.
   ☐ b. Warren bought an airplane ticket.
   ☒ c. Mrs. Angelo told Warren a secret.

2. Which sentence best *characterizes*
   Warren?
   ☐ a. He was very honest and never
       told a lie.
   ☐ b. He loved his wife very much.
   ☒ c. He was looking forward to
       starting a new life far from home.

3. When is "The Angel" *set*?
   ☒ a. on Warren's last day at work
   ☐ b. a week before Warren planned
       to leave the bank
   ☐ c. on Warren's first day at a new job

4. Which sentence best tells the *theme* of
   the story?
   ☐ a. A man who has been stealing
       money from a bank is finally sent
       to jail.
   ☒ b. A man who thinks he has been
       fooling others discovers that he
       has been fooling himself.
   ☐ c. A man who has been working
       very hard for many years is
       rewarded for his efforts.

<table>
<tr><td>☐</td><td>× 5 =</td><td>☐</td></tr>
<tr><td>NUMBER
CORRECT</td><td></td><td>YOUR
SCORE</td></tr>
</table>

EXAMINING VOCABULARY WORDS. Answer the following vocabulary questions by putting an *x* in the box next to the correct answer. The vocabulary words are printed in **boldface** in the story. If you wish, look back at the words before you answer the questions.

1. Mr. Fish told the bank that he would be an hour late because he had an appointment that morning. What is an *appointment*?
   ☒ a. a meeting
   ☐ b. an airplane ticket
   ☐ c. a sore throat

2. Warren said he was going to see a doctor, but he did not go to a medical building. The word *medical* has to do with
   ☐ a. music.
   ☒ b. medicine.
   ☐ c. money.

3. Suddenly Warren grew worried and his voice became shrill. What is the meaning of the word *shrill*?
   ☐ a. very sweet and pleasant
   ☐ b. impossible to hear
   ☒ c. high and sharp in sound

4. Every Friday, Mrs. Angelo came in to make a deposit. As used in this sentence, the word *deposit* means
   ☒ a. money put in a bank.
   ☐ b. a kind of cake.
   ☐ c. a beautiful speech.

	× 5 =	
NUMBER CORRECT		YOUR SCORE

ADDING WORDS TO A PASSAGE. Complete the following paragraph by filling in each blank with one of the words listed in the box below. Each of the words appears in the story. Since there are five words and four blanks, one word in the group will not be used.

In "The Angel," a travel agent got Warren a ___ticket___ to Maui. Maui is one of the ___islands___ in Hawaii.
Did you know that Hawaii is made up of ___more___ than 100 islands? It is a very beautiful state—the only ___one___ that is located in the middle of the Pacific Ocean.

---

ticket   one

more

empty   islands

	× 5 =	
NUMBER CORRECT		YOUR SCORE

74

THINKING ABOUT THE STORY. Each of the following questions will help you to think critically about the selection. Put an *x* in the box next to the correct answer.

1. Which statement is true?
   - ☐ a. Mr. Fowler knew that Warren had been taking money from the bank.
   - ☒ b. Mrs. Angelo found the money that Warren had been hiding.
   - ☐ c. Warren took the 8:25 plane to Maui.

2. It is safe to say that Mrs. Angelo will
   - ☐ a. continue to find a $50 bill every week.
   - ☒ b. not receive any more money from her angel.
   - ☐ c. use a different bank once Warren is no longer there.

3. The fact that Mr. Fish bought a one-way ticket to Hawaii suggests that he
   - ☒ a. didn't plan to come back.
   - ☐ b. often took trips to far-off places.
   - ☐ c. thought he would return home soon.

4. At the end of the story, Warren probably felt
   - ☐ a. amused by how things worked out.
   - ☐ b. pleased that Mrs. Angelo had used the money wisely.
   - ☒ c. upset and disappointed.

Thinking More about the Story. Your teacher might want you to write your answers.

- Warren usually wore gray clothing. But at Greyson's Department Store he bought bright, flowery shirts and white pants. What does this tell you about Warren?
- Why did Warren tell the travel agent that his name was James Strut? Why did he speak in a deeper voice?
- What will Warren discover when he looks for the money he has stored? What might Warren do now?

Use the boxes below to total your scores for the exercises.

☐
+
GETTING THE MEANING OF THE STORY

☐
+
REVIEWING STORY ELEMENTS

☐
+
EXAMINING VOCABULARY WORDS

☐
+
ADDING WORDS TO A PASSAGE

☐
THINKING ABOUT THE STORY

▼

☐ **Score Total:** Story 8

☐ × 5 = ☐

NUMBER CORRECT   YOUR SCORE

9

A White Heron

by Sarah Orne Jewett

The woods were filled with shadows one June evening just before eight o'clock. Light from a bright sunset **shimmered** against the trunks of trees. A little girl named Sylvia was leading her cow home. They were walking away from the light into the dark woods. But they both knew the path very well. It did not matter if they could not see it.

The old cow was stubborn, and smarter than you might have thought. There was hardly a night during the summer when it could be found in the pasture. Instead, it loved to wander far away. Then it would hide itself in the high bushes or among the trees. The cow wore a loud bell. But it discovered that if it stood perfectly still, the bell would not ring.

Then Sylvia had to hunt for the cow. She would call, "Cow! Cow!" over and over until she found it. If the creature had not given plenty of good milk, Sylvia might have grown angry. The truth was that Sylvia had lots of time.

And she had very little use to make of it. So when the weather was good, Sylvia enjoyed searching for the cow. Sylvia thought of it as a game of hide-and-seek. Since there were no children in the area, Sylvia played the game with enthusiasm.

This time, though, the game had lasted nearly three hours. The cow finally gave itself away with a shake of the bell. Sylvia just laughed when she came upon the animal at the edge of a swamp. Now Sylvia used a **twig** of birch leaves to urge the animal in the direction of home.

Sylvia wondered what her grandmother would say because they were so late. A long time had passed since she had left home. But everyone knew that finding the cow was sometimes difficult.

Her grandmother, Mrs. Tilley, had chased after the cow too many evenings to blame anyone else for being late. Mrs. Tilley suspected that

77

Sylvia took her time as she wandered about in the woods and meadows. Mrs. Tilley often said that there never was such a child for straying about out-of-doors. Still, Mrs. Tilley was grateful to have Sylvia's help. As for Sylvia, she felt that she had never been alive at all until she came to live on the farm.

Now Sylvia and the cow were on the shady path at the edge of the woods. The cow stopped at the brook to take a long drink. Sylvia stood still and waited. She let her bare feet cool themselves in the water. Large moths, blind in the fading light, struck softly against her. She waded through the brook as the cow moved on. She listened to the sounds around her with a heart that beat fast with pleasure.

There was a stirring in the tops of the trees. They were full of little birds and animals that seemed to be wide awake and going about their business. Sylvia, herself, felt sleepy as she walked along. However, they were not very far from the house now, and the air was soft and sweet.

Sylvia was not often in the woods as late as this. It made her feel as if she were part of the gray shadows and the flickering leaves. She was thinking how long it seemed since she first came to the farm a year ago. And she was wondering if things were the same in the busy, noisy town she had left.

Suddenly, she was shocked to hear a sharp whistling close by. Before she could take another step, a tall young man stepped onto the path.

"Hello," he called cheerfully. "How far is it to the main road?"

A trembling Sylvia answered softly, "A little way."

She did not dare to look straight at the stranger. He carried a gun over his shoulder. She just walked along and followed the cow. He walked alongside them.

"I have been hunting for some birds," the stranger said kindly. "And I have lost my way and need a friend very much. Don't be afraid," he added. "Speak up and tell me what your name is. I'd like to know if you think I can spend the night at your house. I want to go hunting early in the morning."

Sylvia was more alarmed than before. Would her grandmother think she was to blame? But who could have known this would happen? It did not seem to be her fault. Still, she might be blamed.

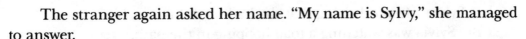

The stranger again asked her name. "My name is Sylvy," she managed to answer.

Mrs. Tilley was standing in the doorway when the three of them came into view. The cow gave a loud moo as if to explain everything.

"Where'd that silly cow hide this time, Sylvy?" asked her grandmother. But Sylvia, still nervous, kept silent.

The young man rested his gun next to the door. Then he wished Mrs. Tilley a good evening and repeated his story. He asked if he could have a night's lodging.

"Put me anywhere you like," he said. "I must be off early in the morning. But I am very hungry, indeed. Anything you might have to eat would do."

"Yes, of course," said Mrs. Tilley. "You might do better if you don't mind walking a mile or so on the main road. But you're welcome to what we've got. I'll find you something to eat right now. You make yourself at home. Now step round and set a plate for the gentleman, Sylvy."

Sylvia stepped promptly. She was glad to have something to do. And she was hungry herself.

Afterward, the gentleman said that this was the best supper he had eaten for a month. Then the three of them sat on the porch while the moon came up.

"Sylvia loves the countryside," grandmother Tilley was saying. "There's not a foot of this land she doesn't know. The wild creatures count her as one of their own. Squirrels come right over and eat out of her hands. The birds do that, too."

The guest suddenly seemed very interested. "So Sylvia knows all about birds, does she?" he exclaimed. "I have been collecting birds ever since I was a little boy. There are two or three very rare ones I have been hunting for the past five years. I mean to get them if they can be found."

"Do you put them in cages?" asked Mrs. Tilley.

"Oh, no. They're stuffed and preserved. I have dozens and dozens of them. And I have shot or caught every one of them myself. I caught a glimpse of a white heron three miles from here on Saturday. I followed it in this direction. They have never been found around here at all." He turned to look at Sylvia. He was hoping that she had seen this rare bird.

But Sylvia was watching a toad hopping in the path.

"You would know the white heron if you saw it," the stranger went on eagerly. "It's a funny, tall, white bird with soft feathers and long, thin legs. And it would have a nest, perhaps at the top of a high tree."

Sylvia's heart skipped a beat. She had seen that strange, white bird. She had once crept softly near where it stood on some green swamp grass. That was way over at the other side of the woods.

"I can't think of anything I would like more than finding that heron's nest," the handsome stranger was saying. "I would give a hundred dollars to anybody who could show it to me. And I plan to spend my whole vacation hunting for it, if necessary."

Mrs. Tilley seemed very interested in all this. But Sylvia silently watched the toad. Later, no matter how she tried, she could not count in her mind the treasures that one hundred dollars would buy.

The next day, the young man wandered about the woods. Sylvia kept him company. She had lost her first fear of the stranger. He told her many things about the birds. And he gave her a pocketknife. She thought of it as a treasure.

Sylvia would have liked him much better without his gun. She could not understand why he killed the very birds he seemed to like so much. Still, she watched him with admiration. She had never seen anyone so charming. The woman's heart, asleep in the child, was somehow thrilled by a dream of love. At last, evening began to fall, and they walked home together.

Half a mile from home, on a high piece of land, stood a tall pine tree. Sylvia had often put her hands on its trunk and looked up at its branches. She had always believed that whoever climbed to the top could see the ocean. Now she thought about the tree. She was filled with excitement. For if she climbed it at dawn, she could see the whole world. She could easily see where the white heron flew. She could watch it closely and find its hidden nest.

What a spirit of adventure! What glory when she later told the secret! It was almost too much for her heart to bear.

Sylvia could not sleep that night. Before morning came, she stole out of the house. She crossed the path through the woods and hurried to the high ground.

There was the huge tree. It was still asleep in the pale moonlight. Sylvia bravely began to climb to the top of it. The way was harder than she thought. She must reach far and hold tightly. The sharp branches caught and held her. They scratched her like angry claws. Still she went higher and higher.

The tree seemed to grow taller and taller as she went up. Still she climbed. Then, finally, she was at the top.

Yes, there was the sea. There were the woodlands and farms. There were churches and white villages. Truly it was a **vast** and enormous world.

The birds sang louder and louder. At last the sun came up. Sylvia could see the white sails of ships at sea. Where was the white heron's nest?

Sylvia looked down toward the green swamp. She had seen it there once. She would see it again. Then look! Look! She saw the white bird rising up like a floating feather. She saw it glide past the pine tree. She saw it come to rest on the branch of a pine tree near her own. She could see its nest!

Satisfied, Sylvia made her way down the tree. She did not dare to look below the branch she stood on. Her fingers ached. She feared she would slip. But over and over, she wondered what the stranger would say. What would he think when she told him how to find his way to the heron's nest?

"Sylvy! Sylvy!" called Mrs. Tilley again and again that morning. But nobody answered. The bed was empty. Sylvia had disappeared.

The guest awoke from a dream and began to dress himself. He thought about the shy little girl. He remembered the way she looked once or twice yesterday. He was sure from those looks that she had seen the white heron. And now she must be persuaded to tell.

Here she comes now, plainer than ever. Her old dress is torn and **tattered** and dirty. The grandmother and the stranger stand in the door. They question her. And now the great moment has come! The time has come to speak of the heron's nest!

But Sylvia does not speak at all. Her grandmother scolds her. And the young man's eyes are looking straight into her own. He can make Sylvia and her grandmother rich with money! He has promised it, and they are poor! He waits to hear the story she has to tell.

No. She keeps silent. What is it that suddenly stops her from telling?

She remembers standing in the green branches. She remembers how the white heron came floating, like a feather, through the golden air. She remembers how they watched the sea together. And Sylvia cannot speak.

She cannot tell the heron's secret. She cannot give its life away.

GETTING THE MEANING OF THE STORY. Complete each of the following sentences by putting an *x* in the box next to the correct answer. Each sentence helps you get the meaning of the story.

1. When Sylvia first saw the stranger, she was
   - ☐ a. pleased because she wanted company.
   - ☐ b. eager to invite him to her home.
   - ☒ c. frightened by him.

2. The stranger asked Mrs. Tilley if
   - ☒ a. he could stay for the night.
   - ☐ b. she could suggest a place to stay nearby.
   - ☐ c. she had seen any rare birds in the neighborhood.

3. Sylvia discovered where the heron's nest was by
   - ☐ a. setting a trap for the heron.
   - ☒ b. climbing a tall tree and seeing where the heron flew.
   - ☐ c. hiding near the swamp and watching the heron.

4. At the end of the story, Sylvia
   - ☐ a. asked the stranger for a hundred dollars.
   - ☐ b. told her grandmother about how she had spent the morning.
   - ☒ c. kept silent.

   [ ] × 5 = [ ]

   NUMBER CORRECT   YOUR SCORE

REVIEWING STORY ELEMENTS. Each of the following questions reviews your understanding of story elements. Put an *x* in the box next to the correct answer to each question.

1. What happened last in the *plot* of the story?
   - ☐ a. Sylvia urged the cow in the direction of home.
   - ☐ b. The stranger gave Sylvia a pocketknife.
   - ☒ c. Sylvia slipped out of the house and headed for the pine tree.

2. Which statement best *characterizes* Sylvia?
   - ☒ a. She loved the out-of-doors and nature.
   - ☐ b. She missed life in the busy, noisy town.
   - ☐ c. She didn't like the creatures of the forest.

3. What is the *setting* of "A White Heron"?
   - ☐ a. a crowded village
   - ☒ b. a farm and the countryside near it
   - ☐ c. a garden in the country

4. Which sentence best tells the *theme* of the story?
   - ☒ a. A young girl decides to give up a large reward to save the life of a beautiful bird.
   - ☐ b. A young girl reveals a secret, and is rewarded with much money.
   - ☐ c. A young girl disappears from home and makes her grandmother very angry.

   [ ] × 5 = [ ]

   NUMBER CORRECT   YOUR SCORE

EXAMINING VOCABULARY WORDS. Answer the following vocabulary questions by putting an *x* in the box next to the correct answer. The vocabulary words are printed in **boldface** in the story. If you wish, look back at the words before you answer the questions.

1. Sylvia used a twig of birch leaves to urge the cow in the direction of home. A *twig* is a
   - ☐ a. long metal pole.
   - ☒ b. small branch.
   - ☐ c. bunch of flowers.

2. The light from the sunset shimmered against the tree trunks. The word *shimmered* means
   - ☒ a. gleamed, or shone, brightly.
   - ☐ b. bothered or annoyed.
   - ☐ c. lifted or raised.

3. From the tree, Sylvia saw a vast and enormous world. What is the meaning of the word *vast?*
   - ☒ a. huge
   - ☐ b. ugly
   - ☐ c. dangerous

4. When Sylvia finished climbing the tree, her dress was torn and tattered. The word *tattered* means
   - ☐ a. new.
   - ☐ b. beautiful.
   - ☒ c. ragged.

ADDING WORDS TO A PASSAGE. Complete the following paragraph by filling in each blank with one of the words listed in the box below. Each of the words appears in the story. Since there are five words and four blanks, one word in the group will not be used.

The heron is a very interesting

_____birds_____ . It has a long neck, long
         1

_____legs_____ , and a long, sharp beak.
       2

The bones in a heron's neck are not all

the _____same_____ size. Therefore when
          3

the heron flies, it _____always_____ holds
                         4

its neck in the shape of the letter S.

> **bird**   **always**
>
> **same**
>
> **pasture**   **legs**

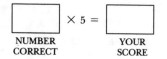
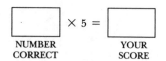

THINKING ABOUT THE STORY. Each of the following questions will help you to think critically about the selection. Put an *x* in the box next to the correct answer.

1. Sylvia knew that if she told the stranger where the heron's nest was, then
   - ☐ a. her grandmother would be upset.
   - ☐ b. the stranger would never visit them again.
   - ☒ c. the heron would be killed.

2. Which one of the following statements is true?
   - ☐ a. Sylvia had climbed the tall pine tree many times before.
   - ☒ b. The stranger was sure that Sylvia had seen the heron.
   - ☐ c. The stranger began collecting birds a short time ago.

3. Clues in the story suggest that the stranger was glad to stay at Mrs. Tilley's house because he
   - ☒ a. had seen the white heron heading in that direction.
   - ☐ b. could not afford to stay anywhere else.
   - ☐ c. had stayed there before and found it comfortable.

4. When the stranger left, he probably felt
   - ☐ a. amused.
   - ☐ b. satisfied.
   - ☒ c. disappointed.

Thinking More about the Story. Your teacher might want you to write your answers.

- Sylvia planned to tell the stranger where the heron's nest was. Then she changed her mind. Explain why. Give at least two reasons.
- At the end of the story, it must have been very difficult for Sylvia to have remained silent. Give reasons to support this statement.
- The stranger would have been willing to give Sylvia five hundred dollars to tell him where the heron's nest was. Do you agree? Explain your answer.

Use the boxes below to total your scores for the exercises.

☐ **G**ETTING THE MEANING OF THE STORY

+

☐ **R**EVIEWING STORY ELEMENTS

+

☐ **E**XAMINING VOCABULARY WORDS

+

☐ **A**DDING WORDS TO A PASSAGE

+

☐ **T**HINKING ABOUT THE STORY

▼

☐ **Score Total:** Story 9

☐ × 5 = ☐

NUMBER
CORRECT

YOUR
SCORE

10

Pop's Boy

by Irvin Ashkenazy

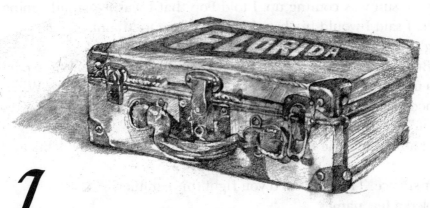

Jt was long after midnight when I hopped off the truck in Lake City, Florida. I dragged my suitcase into an all-night diner. Then I ordered a hamburger.

The only other customer was a thin, elderly man. He was eating a bowl of soup. He stared at me a moment. Then he smiled as he noticed the University of Florida labels on my suitcase.

"Didn't I see you fight in St. Augustine one night last spring?" he asked. "You won the state **amateur** heavyweight title."

I nodded. I was surprised that he recognized me.

"What's your name?" asked the man.

"Jeff Turner," I said.

"You didn't have those scars over your eyes then."

"I turned professional later," I told him. "I needed the money."

"Did you quit school?" the man asked.

"No, I turned pro to stay in school," I said. "To pay my way."

After a while, the old man swung off his stool. "If you're going to the university," he said, "I can take you. I'm going through Gainesville."

As his old car rattled down the road, Pop told stories about the great fighters of the past. He'd been in the business since 1940. He'd been training and managing fighters since then.

"I'm mostly retired now," he said. "But I am looking for someone to fight Kayo Billy Terry tonight. The boxer he was supposed to fight broke his hand yesterday."

By now the sun was coming up. I told Pop that I wasn't actually going to Gainesville. I said I would hitch a ride from there to Miami.

"I thought you were going back to school," he said.

"I was. But first I have to get $500 from a man named Willie. Willie paid the bills for a manager who took me on a tour with some other fighters. When we got finished, Willie disappeared. But I know where he lives in Miami."

"Forget it," Pop said gruffly. "You'll never find him."

I said I had to have the money. I needed $300 to pay off my debts and start school.

Another silence. Then, "Who'd you fight this summer?"

I mumbled a few names.

"You didn't fight *them?* Those are all very tough fighters."

I explained that my manager had put me in pretty good ten-round main fights from the start.

"The rat!" Pop said. "Putting a green kid like you in the ring with guys like those. Did you last ten rounds with any of them?"

I pulled some newspaper clippings from my wallet. Pop nearly wrecked the car, trying to drive and read at the same time.

"Well, I'll be," he said. "You beat 'em all!" After a few moments, he turned to me. "Stay over with me. I'll put you in against Terry tonight. You'll get your $300!"

Pop's landlady glanced at us with an odd, anxious sadness. "Is *he* the one to fight Billy?" she asked Pop.

"He's my boy," Pop said roughly. She gave me something to eat. Then I went to Pop's room to get some sleep.

When I woke up, the windows were filled with night. A stocky, baggy-eyed little man was standing over me. He started rubbing down the muscles in my legs.

"This is J. D., my trainer," Pop explained. "J. D., this is Jeff." We shook hands, and then we headed to the **arena** where the fight was going to be held.

While I was dressing, I told Pop that I'd heard of Kayo Terry a couple of years before. He'd been pretty good. I wondered what he'd done since.

"He's a disgrace to his name," Pop said angrily. "Tonight he's trying to make a comeback. All that means is he'll try to win. That's because nobody's paying him to lose!"

I asked if he could still fight if he wanted to. Pop nodded slowly. "He might have been heavyweight champion, if he'd listened to me." I must have looked surprised. "I used to manage him," Pop muttered.

The roar of the crowd shook the thin walls of the dressing room. "It's almost time to get into the ring," said J. D.

Pop threw an arm over my shoulders. "This boy you're fightin' is good. He can hit and he can box with skill. But he's out of shape. He won't last ten rounds. Hold him off for six rounds and he's through. But until then— watch it! He's tricky and he's dangerous when he fights dirty."

As I moved out at the clang of the bell, Terry charged me, fists flying. He was trying to take me by surprise. I stepped back and took his blows on my gloves and arms. I moved in a circle, letting him tire himself out. Then I caught him with a good jab in the chin.

When he moved back, Terry knew I could box. He must have been worried. He needed to win so badly.

Suddenly, a blinding flash of pain shot through my brain. He had thrust his thumb into my eye. I hunched against the ropes. I couldn't see. While he pounded the back of my head, I managed to get my arms around him. Then I saw stars, as he butted me hard in my forehead. The bell clanged, ending the round.

Pop yelled at the referee about the **foul**. But the referee only shrugged. He hadn't seen it.

The second round started slowly. Terry was trying to save his strength. And I was waiting for him to lose it. The fans grew restless. They began stamping their feet.

Just then Terry rushed me, throwing wild punches. I danced back, but he closed in. Suddenly he grabbed my arms at the elbows, leaned in, and snarled, "Fight!"

For a second I could only stare. I had never before felt hatred toward a man I was fighting. Fear, maybe. But never hatred.

I flung him away from me, clear across the ring. As he bounced back off the ropes, I charged in wildly.

The next thing I knew, a distant voice called, "Six!" I was flat on my back! I was so angry. I hadn't been careful.

"Seven!" called the referee. At "Eight!" I got up on one knee. And at "Nine!" I was on my feet, a bit wobbly.

Terry moved in quickly, trying to finish me. I held on and turned him into the corner. Then, as my head cleared, I made believe I was confused. I pretended to throw a punch, letting my glove go weakly past Terry's head.

Terry charged in confidently. As he did, I drove my left fist against his jaw. He dropped like a stone to the floor.

I was out of the ring by the time the **referee** finished counting to ten. Looking back, I was surprised to see Pop move suddenly into the ring. He lifted Terry in his arms, and dragged him back to the corner.

Pop and I went to a little restaurant afterward. He looked very tired as he handed me a roll of bills. I counted the $300. Then I took $75 and gave it to him.

"What's that for?" he asked. I told him it was his regular manager's share. He pushed the money toward me. "You don't owe me anything, son."

After a while, I said, "He really got me angry. You saw what he was doing in there."

Pop nodded. He wasn't looking at me.

"You planning to finish school?"

I said I guessed so. The question surprised me.

"You do it! Make something of yourself."

J. D. rushed up and said I'd have to hurry to make the bus back to Gainesville. Pop just sat there.

"Aren't you coming to the station with us?" J. D. asked him.

Pop shook his head. "I don't think so. To tell you the truth," he sighed, "I'm kind of worn out."

I grasped his hand. "So long, Pop," I said. "And thanks a million."

At the bus station, J. D. shook my hand. "Pop will get you another fight soon," he said. "You'll make some more easy money."

I said that that night's money hadn't been easy. But it had been the fastest $300 I'd ever made.

J. D. looked puzzled. "What are you talking about?" he asked. "I saw the man at the arena give Pop $100. That was your share."

Before I could say anything else, the bus started up and J. D. pushed me aboard.

The next day, I wrote to Pop. I asked him about the $200 of his own money that he had given me. Later, I wrote two times more. But all my letters came back marked "Not here."

Two months later, J. D. called and offered me a fight in Tampa. He met me at the bus station and hurried me into his car.

"How's Pop?" I asked.

J. D.'s face fell. "Don't you know? Pop's dead."

I felt as though someone had kicked me in the stomach.

I asked when it had happened. He said, "The next morning right after you went back to Gainesville. His landlady found him in bed." J. D. tapped his chest. "Heart just gave out, I guess."

It was a moment or two before I could speak again. "Did Pop have any family?"

"Just that one kid," J. D. said.

"What kid?"

J. D. gave me a surprised look.

"Didn't you know? Billy Terry was Pop's son."

GETTING THE MEANING OF THE STORY. Complete each of the following sentences by putting an *x* in the box next to the correct answer. Each sentence helps you get the meaning of the story.

1. Pop asked Jeff Turner to
   ☐ a. lend him $200.
   ☒ b. fight Billy Terry.
   ☐ c. leave school to become a boxer.

2. According to Pop, Billy Terry
   ☐ a. was once the heavyweight champion.
   ☒ b. was a good fighter who was out of shape.
   ☐ c. could not box very well.

3. The fighter who Jeff knocked out was
   ☐ a. one of Jeff's friends.
   ☐ b. J. D.'s brother.
   ☒ c. Pop's son.

4. The day after Jeff won the fight, Pop
   ☐ a. went back to Gainesville.
   ☐ b. offered Jeff a fight in Tampa.
   ☒ c. died in his bed.

REVIEWING STORY ELEMENTS. Each of the following questions reviews your understanding of story elements. Put an *x* in the box next to the correct answer to each question.

1. What happened first in the *plot* of the story?
   ☐ a. Billy Terry poked Jeff in the eye.
   ☐ b. Pop gave Jeff $300.
   ☒ c. Jeff met Pop in an all-night diner.

2. Which sentence best *characterizes* Pop?
   ☐ a. He always seemed happy and filled with life.
   ☐ b. He was rich because he managed so many famous fighters.
   ☒ c. He was an elderly fight manager who was disappointed in his son.

3. The main action of this story is *set* in a
   ☐ a. car.
   ☒ b. boxing ring.
   ☐ c. restaurant.

4. Which word best describes the *mood* of the story?
   ☒ a. serious
   ☐ b. humorous
   ☐ c. mysterious

	× 5 =	
NUMBER CORRECT		YOUR SCORE

	× 5 =	
NUMBER CORRECT		YOUR SCORE

EXAMINING VOCABULARY WORDS. Answer the following vocabulary questions by putting an *x* in the box next to the correct answer. The vocabulary words are printed in **boldface** in the story. If you wish, look back at the words before you answer the questions.

1. What is the meaning of the word *amateur?*
   - ☐ a. a person who has little power or strength
   - ☐ b. a person who is the star of a movie or play
   - ☒ c. a person who does something for pleasure, not for money

2. Pop and Jeff headed to the arena where the fight was going to be held. What is an *arena?*
   - ☐ a. a very old house
   - ☒ b. a building in which different kinds of contests take place
   - ☐ c. a railroad station

3. When Terry butted Jeff in the forehead, Pop complained about the foul. As used in this sentence, the word *foul* means
   - ☐ a. a ball hit in baseball.
   - ☐ b. a funny smell.
   - ☒ c. something unfair or against the rules.

4. Jeff was out of the ring by the time the referee finished counting to ten. A *referee* is a person who
   - ☒ a. acts as a judge in certain events.
   - ☐ b. trains and manages fighters.
   - ☐ c. buys and sells tickets.

☐	× 5 =	☐
NUMBER CORRECT		YOUR SCORE

ADDING WORDS TO A PASSAGE. Complete the following paragraph by filling in each blank with one of the words listed in the box below. Each of the words appears in the story. Since there are five words and four blanks, one word in the group will not be used.

Almost everyone agrees that boxers must have courage and __skills__ .
     1
Although it is true that ability is needed to box well, __some__ people do not
                    2
consider boxing a sport. They __think__ that boxing should be
      3
banned, or not allowed. They say that boxing is __dangerous__ and cruel. Do
                 4
you have an opinion about this?

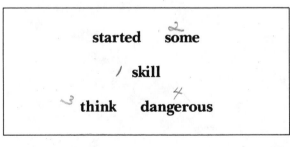

started	**some** (2)
/ **skill**	
(3) **think**	**dangerous** (4)

☐	× 5 =	☐
NUMBER CORRECT		YOUR SCORE

THINKING ABOUT THE STORY. Each of the following questions will help you to think critically about the selection. Put an *x* in the box next to the correct answer.

1. Which statement is true?
   - ☐ a. Billy Terry was a very fair fighter.
   - ☒ b. Jeff made believe he was confused in order to make Terry careless.
   - ☐ c. Pop had been managing fighters for just a few years.

2. Pop said that Terry would try to win because nobody was paying him to lose. This suggests that in the past, Terry
   - ☒ a. purposely lost some fights for money.
   - ☐ b. won every fight he had.
   - ☐ c. always trained very hard for all his fights.

3. Which one of the following shows that Pop still cared about Billy?
   - ☐ a. Pop said that Billy was a disgrace to his name.
   - ☐ b. Pop told Jeff that Billy wouldn't last ten rounds.
   - ☒ c. After Billy was knocked out, Pop lifted him in his arms and helped him back to the corner.

4. How did Jeff probably feel when he discovered that Billy Terry was Pop's son?
   - ☐ a. pleased
   - ☒ b. surprised
   - ☐ c. proud

☐ × 5 = ☐

NUMBER
CORRECT

YOUR
SCORE

Thinking More about the Story. Your teacher might want you to write your answers.

- In this story, the fight manager is called "Pop." Why do you think the author is careful not to tell you Pop's *real* name?
- Who do you think Pop hoped would win the fight? Who do you think he expected to win? Explain your answers.
- Pop died of a broken heart. Do you agree or disagree with this statement? Give reasons to support your answer.

Use the boxes below to total your scores for the exercises.

☐ **G**ETTING THE MEANING OF THE STORY
+
☐ **R**EVIEWING STORY ELEMENTS
+
☐ **E**XAMINING VOCABULARY WORDS
+
☐ **A**DDING WORDS TO A PASSAGE
+
☐ **T**HINKING ABOUT THE STORY
▼
☐ **Score Total:** Story 10

11

Ooka and the Stolen Smell

by I. G. Edmonds

In the days of old Yedo, as Tokyo was once called, storytellers told wonderful tales. Many of the stories were about the wit and wisdom of Ooka Tadasuke.

Ooka was a famous judge. He never refused to hear a complaint. It did not matter if it seemed strange. It did not matter if it seemed foolish. People came to his court with the most unusual cases. But Ooka always agreed to listen to them. And the strangest case of all was the famous "Case of the Stolen Smell."

It all began when a poor student rented a room over a tempura shop. That is a shop where fried food is sold. The student was a poor, young man. Everyone liked him. But the shopkeeper was a **miser.** He suspected one and all of trying to get the better of him. He thought everyone was trying to cheat him.

One day, he heard the student talking with one of his friends.

The friend complained, "It is sad to be so poor that one can afford to eat only plain rice."

"Oh," said the student, "I have found a very fine answer to that problem. Every day, I eat my rice at the same time that the shopkeeper downstairs fries his fish. The smell floats up. That makes my humble rice seem to have much more flavor. It is really the smell, you know, that makes things taste so good."

The shopkeeper was **furious.** To think that someone was enjoying the smell of his fish for nothing!

"Thief!" he shouted to the student. "I demand that you pay me for the smells you have stolen."

"A smell is a smell," the young man answered. "Anyone can smell what he wants to. I will pay you nothing."

The shopkeeper went into a rage. He rushed to Ooka's court. There he charged the student with theft. Of course everyone laughed at him. For how could anyone steal a smell? They thought that Ooka would surely smile and

97

send the man away. But to everyone's surprise, the judge agreed to hear the case.

"All people must be given their hour in court," Ooka explained. "This man feels very strongly about the smells of his food. He feels strongly enough to make a complaint. It is only right that I, as chief judge of the city, should hear the case."

The people in the court smiled. They were amused. But Ooka only frowned at them.

Ooka took his place on the bench. Then he listened very carefully to the evidence. Finally he said, "I have made my decision. There is no doubt that the student is guilty. This is quite clear. Taking another person's property is **theft.** And I cannot see that a smell is different from any other property."

The shopkeeper was delighted. But the student was very upset. He was quite poor. And now he owed the shopkeeper for three months' worth of smelling. He would surely be thrown into prison.

"How much money do you have?" Ooka asked him.

"Only five mon, Your Honor," the boy answered. "And I need that to pay my rent, or I will be thrown out into the street."

"Let me see the money," said the judge.

The young man held out his hand. Ooka nodded. Then he told him to drop the coins from one hand to the other.

The judge listened to the pleasant clink of the money as it bounced from hand to hand.

Then Ooka said to the shopkeeper, "Now you have been paid. If you have any other complaints in the future, please bring them to the court. It is our wish always to be fair."

"But, Your Honor," the shopkeeper protested, "I did not get the money! The thief dropped it from one hand to the other. See. I have nothing! See!" He held up his empty hands.

Ooka looked at him very closely. Then Ooka said, "This court believes that the punishment should fit the crime. I have decided that the price of the *smell* of food shall be the *sound* of money. Therefore, you have been paid. **Justice,** as usual, has been done in my court."

GETTING THE MEANING OF THE STORY.
Complete each of the following sentences
by putting an *x* in the box next to the
correct answer. Each sentence helps you
get the meaning of the story.

. The shopkeeper demanded that the
student pay him for the
☐ a. rice he had eaten.
☒ b. smells he had stolen.
☐ c. fish he had bought.

. Everyone thought that Ooka would
☐ a. decide that the student was
wrong.
☐ b. send the shopkeeper to prison.
☒ c. refuse to listen to the case.

. Ooka asked the student to
☒ a. drop some coins from one hand
to the other.
☐ b. give some money to the
shopkeeper.
☐ c. stop stealing the smells in the
future.

. The judge decided that the price of
the smell of food is
☐ a. five mon.
☐ b. a handful of coins.
☒ c. the sound of money.

REVIEWING STORY ELEMENTS. Each of
the following questions reviews your
understanding of story elements. Put an
x in the box next to the correct answer
to each question.

1. What happened first in the *plot* of
the story?
☒ a. A student rented a room over a
shop where fried food was sold.
☐ b. The judge listened very carefully
to the facts.
☐ c. The shopkeeper rushed to Ooka's
court to complain about the
student.

2. In this story, the *conflict* is between
☐ a. two students.
☒ b. a shopkeeper and a student.
☐ c. a judge and a student.

3. Which sentence best *characterizes* Ooka?
☐ a. He tried to be helpful, but he did
not understand the law very well.
☐ b. He was lazy and foolish.
☒ c. He was wise and clever.

4. What is the *setting* of the story?
☐ a. China, today
☒ b. Tokyo, years ago
☐ c. India, at the present time

[   ] × 5 = [   ]
NUMBER   YOUR
CORRECT   SCORE

[   ] × 5 = [   ]
NUMBER   YOUR
CORRECT   SCORE

EXAMINING VOCABULARY WORDS. Answer the following vocabulary questions by putting an *x* in the box next to the correct answer. The vocabulary words are printed in **boldface** in the story. If you wish, look back at the words before you answer the questions.

1. The shopkeeper was furious and went into a rage. What is the meaning of the word *furious?*
   ☐ a. delighted
   ☐ b. very smart
   ☒ c. very angry

2. The judge said, "Taking another person's property is theft." The word *theft* means
   ☐ a. spending.
   ☒ b. stealing.
   ☐ c. finding.

3. The shopkeeper was a miser; he tried to charge the student for smelling his fish. A *miser* is a person who
   ☒ a. is very cheap and loves money.
   ☐ b. is friendly and helpful to others.
   ☐ c. never complains about anything.

4. Ooka believed that justice, as usual, had been done in his court. Which of the following best defines (gives the meaning of) the word *justice?*
   ☒ a. fair play
   ☐ b. silly actions
   ☐ c. high hopes

	☐	× 5 =	☐
	NUMBER CORRECT		YOUR SCORE

ADDING WORDS TO A PASSAGE. Complete the following paragraph by filling in each blank with one of the words listed in the box below. Each of the words appears in the story. Since there are five words and four blanks, one word in the group will not be used.

Rice is the main _food_ of

many people around the world. In some

countries in Asia, for example, the people

eat rice three times a day. In

those nations, the _people_ eat an

average of 200–300 pounds of rice each

year. In the United States, the average

is much less. It is 6–7 pounds of

rice a year for each person.

people	**food**
room	
rice	**eat**

	☐	× 5 =	☐
	NUMBER CORRECT		YOUR SCORE

THINKING ABOUT THE STORY. Each of the following questions will help you to think critically about the selection. Put an *x* in the box next to the correct answer.

1. It is fair to say that Ooka did not wish to
   - ☐ a. listen to strange or unusual cases.
   - ☒ b. punish the student for his crime.
   - ☐ c. be fair to the shopkeeper.

2. The people in the court probably thought that
   - ☐ a. the student should have been thrown into prison.
   - ☐ b. the shopkeeper should have been given some money.
   - ☒ c. the shopkeeper got what he deserved.

3. When did the student eat his rice?
   - ☐ a. whenever he got hungry
   - ☒ b. when the shopkeeper fried his fish
   - ☐ c. as soon as he arrived home from school

4. At the end of the story, the shopkeeper probably felt
   - ☐ a. amused.
   - ☐ b. pleased.
   - ☒ c. unhappy.

☐ × 5 = ☐

NUMBER CORRECT   YOUR SCORE

Thinking More about the Story. Your teacher might want you to write your answers.

- If you were the judge, would you have let this case come to your court? Give reasons to support your answer.
- Did you agree with what Ooka decided? Explain your answer.
- What lesson or lessons can be drawn from this story? Think of as many as you can.

Use the boxes below to total your scores for the exercises.

☐ GETTING THE MEANING OF THE STORY

+

☐ REVIEWING STORY ELEMENTS

+

☐ EXAMINING VOCABULARY WORDS

+

☐ ADDING WORDS TO A PASSAGE

+

☐ THINKING ABOUT THE STORY

▼

☐ **Score Total:** Story 11

101

12

One Thousand Dollars

by O. Henry

"One thousand dollars," said lawyer Tolman, seriously. He held out his hand. "And here is the money."

Robert Gillian smiled as he took the thin package of new fifty-dollar bills. "It's such an awkward amount," said Gillian to the lawyer. "If it had been ten thousand dollars, it would have been easier. I might have done something really terrific with it. And fifty dollars would have been less trouble."

"You heard the reading of your uncle's will," continued lawyer Tolman. "I don't know if you paid much attention to its details. I must remind you of one. You must give us an account of *exactly* how you have spent this thousand dollars. You must do it as soon as you have spent it all. The will states that clearly. I trust that you will follow your late uncle's wishes."

"You may count on it," said the young man, politely. "I will do it in spite of the extra expense it will cause me. I may have to hire a bookkeeper to help me. I was never very good at figuring accounts."

Gillian went to his club. There he hunted out someone who was known as Bryson.

Bryson was in a corner reading a book. When he saw Gillian approaching, he sighed and put down his book. Then he closed his eyes.

"Wake up, Bryson," said Gillian. "I've got a funny story to tell you."

"I wish you would tell it to someone else," said Bryson. "You know how I hate your stories."

"This is a better one than usual," said Gillian. "And I'm glad to tell it to you. I've just come from my late uncle's lawyer. I learned that my uncle left me exactly one thousand dollars in his will. Now what can a person do with a thousand dollars?"

"I thought," said Bryson, "that your uncle, the late Septimus Gillian, was worth something like half a million dollars."

"He was," agreed Gillian, smiling. "And that's where the joke comes in. He left his entire fortune to science. That is, part of it goes to the person who discovers a new disease. And the rest goes to a hospital for finding a cure for it. There are one or two small gifts on the side. The butler and the housekeeper each get a cheap ring and ten dollars. As for me, I get one thousand dollars."

"You've always had plenty of money to spend," said Bryson.

"Tons," agreed Gillian. "Uncle Septimus was very generous. He gave me an excellent **allowance**."

"Are there any other **heirs**?" asked Bryson.

"No one else was left anything," said Gillian. Gillian frowned. Then he shuffled his feet uneasily. "There is a young woman, a Miss Hayden. She was a **ward** of my uncle and lived in his house. She's quiet, musical—the daughter of somebody who was unlucky enough to be his friend. I forgot to say that she was also left a ring and ten dollars. I wish Uncle Septimus had left me that, too. Then I would have had a ten-dollar lunch. I would have given the waiter the ring as a tip. And I would have had the whole business off my hands." Gillian paused. Then he said, "Tell me, Bryson. What's a fellow to do with one thousand dollars?"

Bryson cleaned his glasses and smiled. And when Bryson smiled, Gillian knew that he was going to be insulting.

"A thousand dollars," said Bryson, "may mean much or little. It depends on the spender. To one person, a thousand dollars may be a fortune. To another, it might be nothing more than pocket change. As for you, Gillian, I suggest you take the money. I suggest you rent a hall for the evening. Then you might lecture your audience—if anyone shows up—on the problems that come from inheriting some money from a wealthy uncle."

"People might like you, Bryson," said Gillian, "if you wouldn't joke so. I asked you to tell me what I could do with a thousand dollars."

"You?" said Bryson, with a gentle laugh. "Why, Bobby Gillian, there's just one thing for you to do. You can go buy Miss Lotta Lauriere a diamond pin with the money. That's my suggestion."

"Thanks," said Gillian, rising. "I thought I could depend upon you, Bryson. You've hit on just the thing! I wanted to spend the money all at once in a lump sum. You see, I've got to turn in an account of how I spend it. And I hate listing things and keeping records."

Gillian called for a cab and said to the driver:

"The stage entrance of the Columbine Theater. Then wait there for me."

Miss Lotta Lauriere was in her dressing room powdering her face. She was getting ready to go on stage at a crowded **matinee**. The stage manager mentioned to her that Mr. Gillian had dropped by.

"Let him in," said Miss Lauriere. "Now what is it, Bobby? I'm going on in two minutes."

"This won't take two minutes. How would you like a little diamond pin? I can pay three zeros with a figure one in front of them."

"Oh, whatever you say," said Miss Lauriere without much interest. "Say, Bobby, did you see that diamond necklace Della Stacey had on the other night? Twelve thousand dollars it cost. But of course—"

"Thirty seconds and you're on," called the stage manager to Miss Lauriere.

"I've got to go now," said Gillian. And he strolled out to where his cab was waiting.

"What would you do if you suddenly found a thousand dollars?" he asked the driver.

"Open a little luncheonette," said the driver, promptly. "I know just the place. I could rake in money with both hands. Now if you were thinking of putting up the cash. . . . "

"Oh, no," said Gillian. "I was just curious. Drive till I tell you to stop. I'll rent your cab by the hour."

Eight blocks down Broadway, Gillian got out. A blind man sat on a stool on the sidewalk selling pencils. Gillian stood before him.

"Excuse me," said Gillian. "But would you mind telling me what you would do if you had a thousand dollars?"

"You got out of that cab that just drove up, didn't you?" asked the blind man.

"I did," said Gillian.

"I thought so," said the blind man. "I could hear the car door slamming shut. Well, then, take a look at this if you like."

He took a small book from his pocket and held it out. Gillian opened it and saw that it was a bank book. It showed a balance of $1,785 in the blind man's account.

Gillian returned the bank book and got back into the cab.

"I forgot something," he said. "You may drive to the law offices of Tolman and Sharp at 39th Street and Broadway."

Lawyer Tolman, a bit surprised, looked curiously at Gillian. "I beg your pardon," said Gillian, cheerfully. "But may I ask you one question? It's not out of order, I hope. Did my uncle leave Miss Hayden anything besides the ring and the ten dollars?"

"Nothing," said Mr. Tolman.

"I thank you very much, sir," said Gillian. And out he went to his cab. He gave the driver the address of his late uncle's home.

Miss Hayden was writing letters in the library. She was small and slender and dressed in black. But you would have noticed her eyes. Gillian drifted in with his air of regarding the world with amusement.

"I've just come from Tolman, the lawyer," Gillian explained. "They've been going over my uncle's papers down there. They found an amendment or something to the will. It seems that my uncle loosened up a little on second thought. He left you a thousand dollars. I was driving up this way and Tolman asked me to bring you the money. Here it is. You'd better count it to see if it's right." Gillian put the money next to her hand on the desk.

Miss Hayden turned pale. "Oh!" she said, and repeated, "Oh!"

Gillian half turned and looked out the window.

After a few moments, he said in a low voice, "I suppose, of course, that you know I love you."

"I am sorry," said Miss Hayden, taking up the money.

"There is no use?" asked Gillian, almost lightly.

"I am sorry," she said again.

"May I write a note?" asked Gillian, with a smile. He seated himself at the big library table. She supplied him with a paper and pen. Then she waited, staring out of the window.

Gillian made out his account of how he had spent the thousand dollars. This is what he wrote:

"Paid by Robert Gillian, the outcast of the family, one thousand dollars to Miriam Hayden, the best and dearest woman on earth."

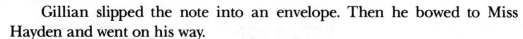

Gillian slipped the note into an envelope. Then he bowed to Miss Hayden and went on his way.

His cab stopped again at the offices of Tolman and Sharp.

"I have spent the thousand dollars," he said cheerfully to Tolman. "And I have come to give you an account of how I have spent it. There is quite a feeling of summer in the air. Don't you think so, Mr. Tolman?" He tossed a white envelope on the lawyer's desk. "You will find a note inside. It tells how I have disposed of the thousand dollars."

Mr. Tolman did not touch the envelope. He went to a door and called his partner, Mr. Sharp. Together they walked to a large safe at the back of the office. From the safe they took a large envelope which was sealed. They opened the envelope and read together the sheet of paper inside. Then Mr. Tolman spoke for them both.

"Mr. Gillian," he said, "there was a *codicil*—an addition—to your uncle's will. It was given to us privately. Your uncle instructed us not to read it until you had given us a written account of how you spent the thousand dollars. As you have done this, my partner and I have read the addition to your uncle's will. I won't bother you with its legal phrases. But I will tell you what it means.

"If you have spent the money in a wise, unselfish, or thoughtful way, we are to hand over to you fifty thousand dollars. This sum of money has been set aside for that purpose. But if you have used this money as you have used money in the past—foolishly and wastefully—the fifty thousand dollars is to be paid to Miriam Hayden without delay. Now, Mr. Sharp and I will read your account of how you spent the thousand dollars."

Mr. Tolman reached for the envelope that Gillian had left on the desk. Gillian was a little quicker, however, in picking it up. Gillian slowly ripped the envelope into pieces. Then he dropped the pieces into his pocket.

"It's all right," Gillian said, smiling. "There's no need to bother you with this. All you would see is a list of bets. I lost the thousand dollars at the race track. Good day, gentlemen."

Tolman and Sharp nodded sadly at each other.

And Gillian, whistling cheerfully, turned on his heels and left.

GETTING THE MEANING OF THE STORY.
Complete each of the following sentences
by putting an *x* in the box next to the
correct answer. Each sentence helps you
get the meaning of the story.

1. Robert Gillian told Miriam Hayden that
   - ☒ a. he loved her.
   - ☐ b. she owed him a thousand dollars.
   - ☐ c. she would receive fifty thousand dollars.

2. Bryson advised Gillian to spend the thousand dollars
   - ☐ a. to open a luncheonette.
   - ☒ b. on a diamond pin for Lotta Lauriere.
   - ☐ c. at the race track.

3. Gillian discovered that the blind man
   - ☐ a. had no money.
   - ☒ b. had $1,785 in the bank.
   - ☐ c. could really see.

4. According to an addition to the will, Gillian would be paid fifty thousand dollars if he
   - ☐ a. became successful in business.
   - ☐ b. married Miss Hayden.
   - ☒ c. spent the thousand dollars unselfishly or thoughtfully.

REVIEWING STORY ELEMENTS. Each of
the following questions reviews your
understanding of story elements. Put an
x in the box next to the correct answer
to each question.

1. What happened last in the *plot* of the story?
   - ☐ a. Gillian visited Lotta Lauriere.
   - ☒ b. Gillian ripped the envelope into pieces.
   - ☐ c. Miss Hayden gave Gillian a pen and paper.

2. Which group of words best *characterizes* Gillian?
   - ☒ a. cheerful, amusing, happy-go-lucky
   - ☐ b. serious, sad, poor
   - ☐ c. selfish, thoughtless, angry

3. Pick the sentence that best tells the *theme* of this story.
   - ☐ a. A man who is disappointed in love gets even with the woman who has turned him down.
   - ☒ b. A young man's actions show that he cares more about the woman he loves than he cares about money.
   - ☐ c. Nothing is more important in life than having a lot of money.

4. Which statement best describes O. Henry's *style* of writing?
   - ☐ a. There is no humor in his stories.
   - ☐ b. His stories are long and very difficult to understand.
   - ☒ c. His stories have surprise endings.

☐ × 5 = ☐

NUMBER CORRECT   YOUR SCORE

☐ × 5 = ☐

NUMBER CORRECT   YOUR SCORE

109

EXAMINING VOCABULARY WORDS. Answer the following vocabulary questions by putting an *x* in the box next to the correct answer. The vocabulary words are printed in **boldface** in the story. If you wish, look back at the words before you answer the questions.

1. Miss Hayden was a ward of Uncle Septimus. As used in this sentence, the word *ward* means
   - ☐ a. a section in a hospital.
   - ☐ b. part of a jail.
   - ☒ c. a person who is under the care of another.

2. Gillian always had plenty to spend because he received a large allowance from his uncle. Which of the following best defines the word *allowance?*
   - ☒ a. a sum of money given regularly
   - ☐ b. an expensive car
   - ☐ c. toys and games

3. Miss Lauriere was getting ready to go on stage at a crowded matinee. What is the meaning of the word *matinee?*
   - ☒ a. an afternoon show
   - ☐ b. a subway car
   - ☐ c. a large store

4. Robert Gillian and Miriam Hayden were named heirs in Uncle Septimus's will. What are *heirs?*
   - ☐ a. wise lawyers
   - ☒ b. people who are left money or property
   - ☐ c. friends or companions

	× 5 =	
NUMBER CORRECT		YOUR SCORE

ADDING WORDS TO A PASSAGE. Complete the following paragraph by filling in each blank with one of the words listed in the box below. Each of the words appears in the story. Since there are five words and four blanks, one word in the group will not be used.

About 600 years ago, Marco Polo, an Italian explorer, _visited_ China. He was very _surprised_ to discover that the people there used paper money. In Italy and _other_ countries around the world, coins were used to pay for goods. The Chinese were probably the first people to make and use _money_ made of paper.

money	visited
	other	
spend	surprised

	× 5 =	
NUMBER CORRECT		YOUR SCORE

110

THINKING ABOUT THE STORY. Each of the following questions will help you to think critically about the selection. Put an *x* in the box next to the correct answer.

1. Why did Gillian say that he lost the thousand dollars at the race track?
   - ☒ a. He wanted Miriam Hayden to receive fifty thousand dollars.
   - ☐ b. He thought he was playing a joke on the lawyers.
   - ☐ c. He was the kind of person who couldn't stop telling lies.

2. We may infer that Gillian ripped up the envelope because he
   - ☐ a. was embarrassed that he lost the money gambling.
   - ☐ b. was very upset that Miss Hayden didn't love him.
   - ☒ c. didn't want the lawyers to read the note he had written.

3. The last sentence of the story suggests that when Gillian left the lawyers, he felt
   - ☒ a. happy.
   - ☐ b. sad.
   - ☐ c. foolish.

4. Which one of the following statements is true?
   - ☐ a. Everyone knew that Miss Hayden was secretly in love with Gillian.
   - ☒ b. Uncle Septimus wanted to reward Gillian for changing.
   - ☐ c. Bryson was always happy to hear Gillian's stories.

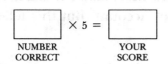

	× 5 =	
NUMBER CORRECT		YOUR SCORE

Thinking More about the Story. Your teacher might want you to write your answers.

- Do you think that Robert Gillian will ever tell Miriam Hayden about how he helped her obtain the fifty thousand dollars? Explain your answer.
- At first, Gillian planned to buy a diamond pin for Lotta Lauriere. Why didn't Gillian buy her the pin?
- At the end of the story, Gillian left the offices of Tolman and Sharp. What do you think the lawyers might have said to each other about Gillian after he was gone?

Use the boxes below to total your scores for the exercises.

	GETTING THE MEANING OF THE STORY
+	
	REVIEWING STORY ELEMENTS
+	
	EXAMINING VOCABULARY WORDS
+	
	ADDING WORDS TO A PASSAGE
+	
	THINKING ABOUT THE STORY
▼	
	Score Total: Story 12

13

Setup

by Jack Ritchie

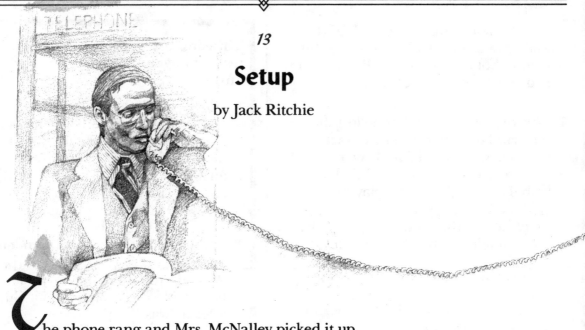

The phone rang and Mrs. McNalley picked it up.

"Hello?" she said.

The voice was a man's. It said, "Is this Mrs. Andrea McNalley?"

"Yes."

"Well, then, my name is Mr. Hamilton. James Hamilton. I am a vice-president at the First National Bank in the Southview Shopping Center."

Mrs. McNalley was tall and slender and in her sixties. She nodded to herself. Then she said, "That's my bank."

"Yes," said Mr. Hamilton. "Mrs. McNalley," he went on, "I've heard that you are a respected citizen in this community. A person who can be trusted."

"I guess so," said Mrs. McNalley. "Why?"

"I . . . that is . . . *we* would like your help, Mrs. McNalley. We need your cooperation."

"What's the trouble?"

"We have an **employee**—a teller at our bank who. . . . How shall I put it? We are *suspicious* of him."

"What's he been up to?"

"We think he's been changing his records, Mrs. McNalley. For example, a customer takes seven hundred dollars out of an account. But this teller

112

marks the withdrawal as being *eight* hundred dollars. Then he pockets the extra one hundred dollars for himself."

"Sounds like a pretty foolish thing to do. Why isn't he behind bars, Mr. Hamilton?"

"He is very clever, very clever, Mrs. McNalley. Somehow he has a way of covering up the difference. He does it before we can check on his books at the end of the day. It's all very technical, Mrs. McNalley. It would take a long time to explain. However, we—the officers of the bank and I—have talked about this case many times. And we have decided on the best way to catch this **criminal**. That would be to catch him while he was in the *act* of **committing** the crime."

"I suppose so," said Mrs. McNalley. "But where do I come in?"

"You have . . . let me see. I have your records somewhere here on my desk. You have something like $10,000 in your savings account?"

"$5,256 and a few cents," Mrs. McNalley said.

"Ah, yes. I have the records now. $5,256. And those extra pennies. But they do add up, don't they?"

"Which teller is it?" asked Mrs. McNalley. "There are three or four tellers at the bank."

"I don't think I ought to mention his name. However, I can tell you this. He's a young man in his late twenties. He has black hair and a mustache."

"Oh, sure," Mrs. McNalley said. "I know who you mean. I never did trust him. I know you can't judge a book by its cover. But I just don't like him."

"No," said Mr. Hamilton, "you can't judge a book by its cover. But this time, you seem to be right."

Mr. Hamilton paused. Then he went on. "Now, ma'am, it is just after 10:00 A.M. We—the officers of the bank and I—would like you to go to this teller's window at exactly eleven o'clock. We would like you to withdraw $5,000 from your account."

"Five thousand dollars?"

"We are not asking you to go through all this trouble for *nothing,* Mrs. McNalley. We will see that you receive two hundred dollars. We will give you that for your help in catching this criminal."

"Two hundred dollars?" There was a pause. "If I take out $5,000, what then?"

"Put the bills into an envelope and leave the bank. Then walk to that little park in the shopping center."

"The park in Darrow Square?"

"Yes, that's the one. Anyway, go there and sit on one of the benches. Just wait for me. I should be there in five or ten minutes."

"Should I sit on any particular bench?"

"Any one will do. I'll recognize you. When I join you, give me the envelope."

"Give you the envelope?"

"Yes. You see, that is *evidence.* We will need it."

"But . . ."

"You have nothing at all to worry about, Mrs. McNalley. Our bank will cover you for the entire amount. It's just something we must do to satisfy the law. We need the money when the police make the arrest. I will return the money to you immediately after. The whole thing shouldn't take more than half an hour. And remember, we'll give you two hundred dollars for your help. That's not bad for the loan of $5,000 for half an hour. Not bad at all, is it, Mrs. McNalley?"

114

"Do you want me to stay in Darrow Square until you come back with the money?"

"Exactly, Mrs. McNalley. You stay there until I get back."

The man who called himself Mr. Hamilton had telephoned from a phone booth. The phone booth was in a luncheonette. He waited for three minutes. Then he dialed Mrs. McNalley's number again.

Mrs. McNalley answered. "Hello?"

Hamilton was good at changing his voice. "Is Bill there?" he asked.

"Bill? There's no Bill here."

"Isn't this 555-4778?"

"No. This is 555-4779."

"Sorry. I must have dialed the wrong number."

He waited another three minutes. Then he dialed Mrs. McNalley's number once more. He heard Mrs. McNalley's phone ring. Then he hung up.

Good. The line hadn't been busy either time he dialed.

If the suckers didn't phone the police in the first five or six minutes, chances were they had been hooked. It meant that they had believed his story.

Hamilton sat down at a booth near the window. He ordered a sandwich. From where he was sitting, he could watch the front of Mrs. McNalley's apartment building. He always liked being able to do that. It made him feel safer. More than once he had seen a police car drive up. That happened when the sucker got suspicious later and phoned the police.

Hamilton ate his sandwich.

Why did they fall for his story so often? He wasn't sure.

Yesterday morning Hamilton had gone to the Southview Shopping Center. He had spent two hours in the First National Bank there. He kept an eye on the customers that came in. Finally, he selected Andrea McNalley. She seemed to be at least sixty-five and was very well dressed.

When Mrs. McNalley left the bank that morning, Hamilton stayed not far behind. Mrs. McNalley walked four blocks. Then she went into her apartment building.

Hamilton found out Mrs. McNalley's name. He had his own way of doing this. Then he found out her phone number.

Now, Hamilton finished eating his sandwich. He looked out the window toward the apartment house. He glanced at his watch. Then he saw Mrs. McNalley leave the apartment building. She began walking toward the shopping center. She was going to the bank.

Hamilton quickly paid his bill. Then he left. He was a block behind Mrs. McNalley when she entered the bank.

After about ten minutes, Mrs. McNalley came out of the bank. She headed toward the park. Once there, she looked at the benches. Then she sat down on one of them.

Hamilton waited another five minutes. Then he approached. "Mrs. McNalley?" he asked.

Mrs. McNalley looked up. "Mr. Hamilton? The vice-president of the bank?"

Hamilton nodded. "Do you have the money?"

Mrs. McNalley took an envelope from her pocketbook. "You said something about two hundred dollars?"

"Of course." Hamilton took out his wallet. He removed two one hundred dollar bills. "Here you are, ma'am. And the bank wishes to thank you for your **cooperation**."

Hamilton glanced into the envelope. The money was all there. "Now I'll go back to the bank. We'll take care of that teller immediately. I should be back in half an hour."

He took a dozen steps. Then he felt a tap on his shoulder. He turned to face a tall man. Hamilton knew at once that the man was a detective.

The tall man spoke. "You are under arrest," he told Hamilton. "You have the right to remain silent. You have the right to. . . . "

Hamilton closed his eyes and listened in silence.

Moments later, Mrs. McNalley joined them. She turned to Hamilton.

"I waited *fifteen* minutes before I called the police," she said. Mrs. McNalley smiled. "I spent thirty years on the police force before I retired. During that time, I learned every trick that crooks like you pull. I knew this one well."

"Let's be going," the detective told Hamilton. Hamilton sighed. Someone had once told him that crime didn't pay.

GETTING THE MEANING OF THE STORY.
Complete each of the following sentences
by putting an *x* in the box next to the
correct answer. Each sentence helps you
get the meaning of the story.

. Mr. Hamilton wanted Mrs. McNalley to
  ☒ a. give him an envelope with
      $5,000.
  ☐ b. complain to the bank about a
      teller.
  ☐ c. meet him at a luncheonette.

. For helping the bank, Hamilton
  promised to give Mrs. McNalley
  ☐ a. a letter of thanks.
  ☐ b. free lunch at the bank.
  ☒ c. two hundred dollars.

. Hamilton called back twice because
  he wanted to
  ☐ a. tell Mrs. McNalley something he
      had forgotten.
  ☒ b. make sure Mrs. McNalley wasn't
      on the phone talking to the
      police.
  ☐ c. remind her to go to the bank at
      eleven o'clock.

. After Hamilton spoke to her on the
  phone, Mrs. McNalley
  ☐ a. went immediately to the bank.
  ☐ b. called a detective at once.
  ☒ c. waited fifteen minutes and then
      called the police.

REVIEWING STORY ELEMENTS. Each of
the following questions reviews your
understanding of story elements. Put an
x in the box next to the correct answer
to each question.

1. What happened last in the *plot* of
  the story?
  ☐ a. Mrs. McNalley waited on a bench
      in the park.
  ☒ b. A tall man tapped Mr. Hamilton
      on the shoulder.
  ☐ c. Hamilton looked out the window
      and watched the apartment house.

2. Which sentence best *characterizes* James
  Hamilton?
  ☐ a. He was a vice-president at a bank
      and could be trusted.
  ☒ b. He was a crook who stole people's
      savings.
  ☐ c. He was very friendly because he
      liked people so much.

3. "You are under arrest. You have the
  right to remain silent." These lines of
  dialogue were spoken by
  ☒ a. a detective to Mr. Hamilton.
  ☐ b. Mr. Hamilton to Mrs. McNalley.
  ☐ c. Mrs. McNalley to Mr. Hamilton.

4. Which sentence best tells the *theme* of
  the story?
  ☒ a. A woman "turns the tables" on
      a man who tries to trick her.
  ☐ b. A teller at a bank is caught stealing.
  ☐ c. A woman loses $5,000 to a clever
      thief.

	× 5 =	
NUMBER CORRECT		YOUR SCORE

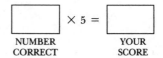

	× 5 =	
NUMBER CORRECT		YOUR SCORE

117

EXAMINING VOCABULARY WORDS. Answer the following vocabulary questions by putting an *x* in the box next to the correct answer. The vocabulary words are printed in **boldface** in the story. If you wish, look back at the words before you answer the questions.

1. Mr. Hamilton said that an employee at the bank seemed to be changing bank records. Which of the following is the meaning of the word *employee?*
   - ☒ a. a worker
   - ☐ b. a customer
   - ☐ c. a guest

2. They hoped to catch the teller while he was in the act of committing the crime. The word *committing* means
   - ☐ a. enjoying.
   - ☒ b. doing.
   - ☐ c. driving to.

3. Hamilton told Mrs. McNalley that the bank was grateful to her for her cooperation. The word *cooperation* means
   - ☒ a. working together.
   - ☐ b. cheerful manner.
   - ☐ c. large sum of money.

4. The officers at the bank thought of a plan to catch the criminal. A *criminal* is a person who has
   - ☐ a. been absent often.
   - ☐ b. argued loudly with others.
   - ☒ c. broken the law.

	× 5 =	
NUMBER CORRECT		YOUR SCORE

ADDING WORDS TO A PASSAGE. Complete the following paragraph by filling in each blank with one of the words listed in the box below. Each of the words appears in the story. Since there are five words and four blanks, one word in the group will not be used.

In France, police officers are called *gendarmes*. In England, _police_ officers are known as *bobbies*. In the United States, of course, police officers are often _called_ "cops." How did they get this _name_? It comes from the copper buttons that were once _found_ on police uniforms.

> **called**   **benches**
>
> **police**
>
> **found**   **name**

	× 5 =	
NUMBER CORRECT		YOUR SCORE

THINKING ABOUT THE STORY. Each of the following questions will help you to think critically about the selection. Put an x in the box next to the correct answer.

1. Which one of the following statements is true?
☐ a. Mrs. McNalley was fooled by Mr. Hamilton.
☐ b. Mr. Hamilton enjoyed working at the First National Bank.
☒ c. The teller at the bank wasn't really stealing money.

2. It is safe to say that Mr. Hamilton planned to
☐ a. return the money to Mrs. McNalley.
☐ b. see that the teller was sent to jail.
☒ c. disappear with the money.

3. Why did Hamilton change his voice when he asked to speak to Bill?
☐ a. He wanted to surprise Bill.
☒ b. He didn't want Mrs. McNalley to know who he was.
☐ c. He wanted to see if Bill could guess who he was.

4. This story suggests that you should
☒ a. be on guard when a stranger offers you money over the phone.
☐ b. keep your savings at home and not in a bank.
☐ c. always carry a large amount of cash with you.

☐ × 5 = ☐

NUMBER
CORRECT

YOUR
SCORE

Thinking More about the Story. Your teacher might want you to write your answers.

● Mr. Hamilton said that you can't judge a book by its cover. Show how this was true of Hamilton himself.
● Even if Mrs. McNalley hadn't tricked Hamilton, sooner or later he would surely have been caught. Discuss this statement.
● What lesson or lessons can be drawn from this story? Think of as many as you can.

Use the boxes below to total your scores for the exercises.

☐ GETTING THE MEANING OF THE STORY
+
☐ REVIEWING STORY ELEMENTS
+
☐ EXAMINING VOCABULARY WORDS
+
☐ ADDING WORDS TO A PASSAGE
+
☐ THINKING ABOUT THE STORY
▼
☐ **Score Total:** Story 13

14

The Woodcutter's Child

by Manuela Williams Crosno

"How is it," Gomez asked his wife, "that the Verlados have a child with hair like gold?"

This *had* come about in a strange way. This is the story.

$\mathcal{E}$nrique Verlado was a woodcutter. He lived with his wife, Maria, in a cabin he had built at the edge of a small canyon. Crops were planted in a narrow valley between the canyon walls. A stream, fresh from the mountains, brought water to these fields.

Morning glories, with large blue blossoms, trailed around the cabin windows. Pink and white hollyhocks grew beside the wall. Pots of red geraniums stood in the windows. There were lace curtains behind them.

Soon after the woodcutter married, the canyon began to glow with a bronze color at each sunset. This may have been caused by the sunlight. It was reflected against the rust and orange rocks of the east canyon wall. The whole valley—grass, cabin, trees, the stream, even Maria and Enrique—became a copper painting at sunset.

Near the top of the canyon wall was a narrow road. Sometimes, those who traveled this road would look into the canyon at sunset. Then they would exclaim, "Look! A bronze cabin! How beautiful!"

Maria and Enrique traveled their own path and dreamed their own dreams. One of those dreams was to have a child. As they danced and sang, they told themselves there would be children, *niños,* one day. The canyon walls echoed with happy laughter.

Enrique spent most of his days in the forest. He would thin out the brush, or chop down dead trees. These he sold for firewood in a nearby village. Sometimes, he would lie under a tree and watch the sky through the pine needles. The wind blew soft and golden clouds across the mesas.

"There is no better place than this to raise a child," Enrique often said. Maria and Enrique were very happy.

As time passed, however, they laughed less and smiled seldom. Finally, they no longer smiled at all. This was because they had no children. Gomez, who lived near them, had seven *niños,* all with straight, blue-black hair and shiny-black eyes. But Maria and Enrique Verlado had not even one child.

Sadness aged them, and the days dragged slowly by. The lace curtains became torn and stained. Sand filled the garden. The hollyhocks came up thin and **frail**, in ones and twos. The geraniums wilted at the window sills. And no blue morning glories brightened the cabin.

One evening as Maria was herding goats toward the corral, she found, on the grass, a yellow scarf. It gleamed like sunshine. Now and then, something fell into the canyon from the high road above. But this scarf looked as though it had traveled a great distance—like a seed which has been carried by the wind. Indeed, Maria did find a seed tied tightly in a corner of the scarf.

Maria held the seed in her hand and examined it closely. She decided that it was a hollyhock seed. Then she planted it in the garden close to the cabin door.

The scarf seemed to be woven of a shimmering silk. Maria wrapped it around her hair. When Enrique came home, she told him about the seed. With the bright yellow scarf on her black hair, Maria looked very beautiful.

In a few days, a green stalk appeared in the garden where the seed had been planted. Maria took a great interest in this seedling. She was reminded of hollyhocks she had planted in happier days.

Maria watered the stalk and put fresh soil around its roots. She carefully removed the old, sandy soil which makes a plant struggle to live. It seemed to Maria that this hollyhock was different from any she had ever planted.

This strange plant brought a new delight to the woodcutter and his wife. But they did not mention the plant to their neighbor, Gomez. Some years before, he had said that the Verlados raised hollyhocks instead of children. This had saddened and angered Maria and Enrique.

Before long, the hollyhock reached above the roof of the cabin. The plant had many branches with small buds. When they blossomed one day, the flowers shone brightly in the sunlight. Maria noticed that the flowers were the same color as the yellow scarf she wore.

So the plant was not a hollyhock after all! Its blossoms were like cups of fluffy gold, the color of clouds at sunset. Maria and Enrique were strangely happy. Once more the canyon walls echoed with their laughter.

Late one night, when only the wind was moving, there came a knocking at the door. The woodcutter opened it and looked about. Seeing nothing, he returned to his bed. As Enrique watched the moonlight make patterns on the floor, he wondered what the sound could have been. Just then, he heard the knocking again. Enrique hurried to the door and opened it. He looked about until his eyes became **accustomed** to the moonlight. Near the door he found a basket, which he took into the cabin.

He called Maria. Together they removed a baby from the basket.

The woodcutter dressed hastily and went outside to look about. At the same time, Maria began to care for the child. The baby was wrapped in a golden blanket. It seemed to Maria that the blanket was made of the same material as the scarf. It was surely the same color. As for the basket, Maria had never seen one like it before. Its color was bronze.

Outside, Enrique heard nothing but the soft "swishhh" of wind in the pines. He could see or hear nothing unusual. But the moonlight! Never before had he seen moonlight fill the canyon with the color of sunset bronze. Puzzled, Enrique ran his fingers through his curly, black hair. Could it be that his eyes were **deceiving** him? He walked down the path for a distance. The breeze seemed to be filled with the scent of golden flowers. Seeing no one, Enrique returned to the cabin.

The baby, a boy, was very beautiful. He had blue eyes and fair skin. His hair was the color of golden flowers. It lay in curls all over his head.

Maria and Enrique knew at once that they wanted to keep the child forever. For weeks, indeed months, they kept the baby out of sight. They trembled whenever a stranger approached the cabin.

Finally, they felt certain that the child belonged to them. They reasoned that it had come about, somehow, because of the scarf, the seed, and the golden plant. It was difficult to understand. But somehow they had been given what they wanted most. This was not an abandoned baby left at their doorstep! This child had been given to them. It was really theirs!

One night Maria dreamed that the child's name was *Felicidad*. This was their word for happiness. No longer afraid now, they told everyone that Felicidad was their child.

When Gomez saw the baby, however, he became suspicious. "This boy does not belong to the Verlados," he told his wife. There were whispers, started by Gomez, that Enrique and Maria had stolen the child. But the woodcutter and his wife refused to allow themselves to be worried.

"Happiness," Maria said, "cannot be taken from those who appreciate it."

A year quickly passed by. Except for Gomez, people stopped saying that the baby was not theirs. And Maria and Enrique no longer worried that someone would suddenly appear to claim the child.

Never before had the woodcutter and his wife been so happy. By day white clouds floated over the canyon. And at sunset the bronze color came and went. Maria smiled while she worked with the child close by. Enrique sang all day as he cut the wood.

Maria made new curtains and replaced the geraniums. Enrique painted the window frames blue and repaired his wagon. Life was good in the canyon.

The days were blown away with the speed of winds. Soon three years had passed. Maria and Enrique wanted nothing more. They did not think it strange that the child did not speak. For the little boy with the golden hair smiled and laughed a great deal.

One day the woodcutter arrived home early. He did not have his usual song and smile of greeting. Maria did not question Enrique while they ate. She sat in silence and looked out the window. She noticed that, for the first time, the sun did not color the canyon. Maria found this puzzling. But she did not mention it to her husband.

After the child was asleep, she asked, "What's wrong? What's going on?"

"It is Gomez," said Enrique in an angry voice. "He is saying that if the child is ours, why do we not have more children. I wish for another child!"

Maria tried to comfort Enrique. She replied, "It does not matter what anyone says. Are we not happy—more happy than Gomez with all his children? Ask Gomez why *he* does not have a child with hair like gold."

Nervously, Maria removed her scarf and twisted it. Then she looked at the scarf, knotted in her hands. She wondered if it were beginning to fade.

But Enrique would not be comforted. And he would not forget what Gomez had said. It bothered him more and more. Maria, too, began to wish for another child. This would make her husband content.

And so the woodcutter and his wife grew unhappy again. The lace curtains began to fade. Sand filled the garden once more. The geraniums began to wilt. And Maria began to **neglect** the golden plant near the door. She did not water it for days. She forgot to give it fresh soil.

The sun shone on the canyon wall. But the bronze glow had disappeared, and the canyon seemed dreary and dull. And one morning, the plant with the flowers of gold was found suddenly uprooted.

With each day, the woodcutter and his wife grew sadder. Still, Felicidad remained cheerful. But even the boy could no longer bring them happiness. It served to remind them that they had only one child.

One night, Enrique was awakened by a hand tugging at his sleeve. A startled Maria was speaking to him.

"Come with me," she said. She took him by the hand and drew him to the child's room. When they entered, Enrique saw an empty bed.

They dashed to the door and threw it open. As far down the road as they could see, there was nothing. The breeze stirred the pine needles, and the moon shone between the passing clouds.

The woodcutter and his wife stood silently in the doorway without moving. It was as if they were changed to stone.

Felicidad was gone!

GETTING THE MEANING OF THE STORY.
Complete each of the following sentences
by putting an *x* in the box next to the
correct answer. Each sentence helps you
get the meaning of the story.

1. As Maria was herding goats one
   evening, she found a
   ☐ a. hat.
   ☒ b. scarf.
   ☐ c. pot of flowers.

2. For months, the Verlados kept the child
   hidden because they
   ☒ a. were afraid that someone would
        claim him.
   ☐ b. didn't want anyone to see how
        weak and sickly he was.
   ☐ c. thought that the baby would be
        frightened by strangers.

3. Gomez told people that Maria
   and Enrique
   ☐ a. were very happy.
   ☐ b. would soon leave the canyon.
   ☒ c. had stolen the child.

4. As the woodcutter and his wife grew
   sadder, Felicidad
   ☐ a. also grew sadder.
   ☐ b. refused to eat.
   ☒ c. remained cheerful.

REVIEWING STORY ELEMENTS. Each of
the following questions reviews your
understanding of story elements. Put an
x in the box next to the correct answer
to each question.

1. Where is "The Woodcutter's Child" *set?*
   ☒ a. in a canyon
   ☐ b. on a mountaintop
   ☐ c. in a desert

2. What happened last in the *plot* of the story?
   ☐ a. Maria planted the seed she found.
   ☒ b. The woodcutter and his wife dis-
        covered that Felicidad was gone.
   ☐ c. Enrique and Maria began to wish
        for another child.

3. Which sentence best *characterizes* both
   Maria and Enrique?
   ☐ a. They never smiled or sang
        because they were poor and life
        was hard.
   ☒ b. They were filled with happiness
        during their first three years with
        Felicidad.
   ☐ c. They did not think that they lived
        in a good place to raise a child.

4. Pick the sentence that best tells the
   theme of the story.
   ☐ a. Bright flowers and lace curtains help
        to cheer up an unhappy couple.
   ☐ b. A scarf brings a couple bad luck.
   ☒ c. When a couple cannot be satisfied
        with the happiness they have been
        given, they lose that happiness.

	× 5 =	
NUMBER CORRECT		YOUR SCORE

	× 5 =	
NUMBER CORRECT		YOUR SCORE

EXAMINING VOCABULARY WORDS. Answer the following vocabulary questions by putting an *x* in the box next to the correct answer. The vocabulary words are printed in **boldface** in the story. If you wish, look back at the words before you answer the questions.

1. The flowers in the garden came up weak and frail. Which of the following best defines (gives the meaning of) the word *frail*?
   - ☐ a. in good health
   - ☒ b. easily broken
   - ☐ c. huge

2. Enrique was puzzled, and wondered if his eyes were deceiving him. The word *deceiving* means
   - ☒ a. tricking.
   - ☐ b. approaching.
   - ☐ c. asking.

3. Maria began to neglect the plant near the door; she did not water it for days. What is the meaning of *neglect*?
   - ☐ a. to give praise to
   - ☐ b. to take good care of
   - ☒ c. to fail to care for

4. The woodcutter looked about until his eyes became accustomed to the light. The word *accustomed* means
   - ☒ a. familiar with or used to.
   - ☐ b. upset with or troubled by.
   - ☐ c. surprised by or shocked at.

	× 5 =	
NUMBER CORRECT		YOUR SCORE

ADDING WORDS TO A PASSAGE. Complete the following paragraph by filling in each blank with one of the words listed in the box below. Each of the words appears in the story. Since there are five words and four blanks, one word in the group will not be used.

A deep valley with steep sides is called a *canyon* . Some canyons are famous because they are so *beautiful*₂ to look at. One of these is the Grand Canyon in Arizona. As the light changes during the day, the colors of the many *rocks*₃ there also change. They glisten orange, pink, *yellow*₄, green, and red in the sun.

> **beautiful**   **canyon**
>
> **yellow**
>
> **cabin**   **rocks**

	× 5 =	
NUMBER CORRECT		YOUR SCORE

THINKING ABOUT THE STORY. Each of the following questions will help you to think critically about the selection. Put an *x* in the box next to the correct answer.

1. Probably, the Verlados were afraid that people might think that the baby was not theirs because
   - ☐ a. Maria and Enrique always said that they didn't want any children.
   - ☐ b. everyone knew that the Verlados couldn't afford to support a child.
   - ☒ c. Maria and Enrique had black hair, but the baby had golden curls.

2. Which statement is true?
   - ☒ a. Gomez was not a good neighbor.
   - ☐ b. Gomez was a very helpful neighbor.
   - ☐ c. From the moment they saw the baby, Maria and Enrique did not like it.

3. When the Verlados grew unhappy, they
   - ☐ a. went to dances to cheer themselves up.
   - ☒ b. no longer took good care of their home and their garden.
   - ☐ c. worked harder than ever to keep themselves busy.

4. Probably, Maria and Enrique will
   - ☐ a. see Felicidad one more time.
   - ☐ b. see Felicidad often in the future.
   - ☒ c. never see Felicidad again.

	× 5 =	
NUMBER CORRECT		YOUR SCORE

Thinking More about the Story. Your teacher might want you to write your answers.

- The child in the story is named *Felicidad,* the Spanish word for "happiness." Why do you think the author chose this name? Explain your answer in detail.
- If Enrique and Maria had remained happy, do you think Felicidad would have disappeared? Explain your answer.
- The colors bronze, yellow, and gold play an important part in "The Woodcutter's Child." Give examples from the story to support this statement.

Use the boxes below to total your scores for the exercises.

	GETTING THE MEANING OF THE STORY
+	
	REVIEWING STORY ELEMENTS
+	
	EXAMINING VOCABULARY WORDS
+	
	ADDING WORDS TO A PASSAGE
+	
	THINKING ABOUT THE STORY

▼

Score Total: Story 14

15

Gold-Mounted Guns

by F. R. Buckley

*E*vening had fallen on Longhorn City. A hard-faced man walked down the main street and got a pony from the dozen hitched beside Tim Geogehan's general store. From the dark the hard-faced man heard himself called by name.

"Tommy!"

The hard-faced man made a very slight movement toward his low-slung belt. But it was a movement well known by the man in the shadows.

"Wait a minute!" the voice pleaded.

A moment later his hands upraised, a young man moved into the open.

"Don't shoot," he said. "I'm a friend."

For perhaps fifteen seconds the new-comer and the hard-faced man looked at each other. Then the man with the gun said, "What do you want?"

"Can I put my hands down?" asked the other.

"All things being equal," he said, "I think I'd rather you'd first tell me how you got round to calling me Tommy. Been asking people in the street?"

"No," said the boy. "I only got into town this afternoon, and I ain't a fool any-way. I seen you ride in this afternoon. The way folks backed away from you made me wonder who you was. Then I see them gold-mounted guns, and of course I knew. Nobody ever had guns like them but Pecos

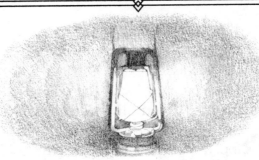

Tommy. I could have shot you while you was getting your horse, if I'd been that way inclined."

The lean man bit his moustache.

"Put 'em down. What do you want?"

"I want to join you."

"You want to *what?*"

"Yeah, I know it sounds foolish to you, maybe," said the young man. "But, listen—your sidekick's in jail down in Rosewell. I figured I could take his place—anyway, till he got out. I know I ain't got any record, but I can ride and I can shoot. And—I got a little job to bring into the firm to start with."

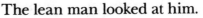

The lean man looked at him.

"Have, eh?" he asked, softly.

"It ain't anything like you go in for as a rule," said the boy, "but it's a roll of cash and—I guess it'll show you I'm straight. I only got on to it this afternoon. It's good I should meet you right now."

The lean man chewed his moustache. His eyes did not shift.

"Yeah," he said, slowly. "What you quitting punching for?"

"Sick of it."

"Figuring robbing trains is easier money?"

"No," said the young man, "I ain't. But I like a little spice in life. There ain't none in punching."

129

"Got a girl?" asked the lean man.

The boy shook his head.

"Well, what's the job?" he asked.

"If you're going to take me on," said the young man, "I can tell you while we're riding toward it. If you ain't, why, there's no need to go no further."

The older man slipped back into its holster the gold-mounted gun he had drawn. Then he turned his pony and mounted.

"Come on," he commanded.

Five minutes later the two had passed the limits of the town. Will Arblaster had given the **details** of his job to the man at his side.

"How do you know the old guy's got the money?"

"I saw him come out of the bank this afternoon, grinning all over his face and stuffing it into his pants pocket," said the boy. "And when he was gone, I kind of inquired who he was. His name's Sanderson, and he lives in this cabin about a mile ahead. Looked kind of a soft old geezer—kind that'd give up without any trouble. Must have been quite some cash there, judging by the size of the roll. But I guess when *you* ask him for it, he won't mind letting it go."

"I ain't going to ask him," said the lean man. "This is your job."

The boy hesitated.

"Well, if I do it right," he asked, "will you take me along with you sure?"

"Yeah—I'll take you along."

The two ponies rounded a shoulder of the hill. Before the riders there was the dark shape of a cabin, its windows unlighted. The lean man chuckled.

"He's out."

Will Arblaster swung off his horse.

"Maybe," he said, "but likely the money ain't. He started off home, and if he's had to go out again, likely he's hid the money someplace. Folks know *you're* about. I'm going to see."

He crept toward the house, and the darkness swallowed him. The lean man, sitting on his horse, motionless, heard the rap of knuckles on the door. A moment later there came the heavy **thud** of a shoulder against wood—

130

a cracking sound, and a crash as the door went down. The lean man's lips tightened. In the quiet, out there in the night, the man on the horse, twenty yards away, could hear the clumping of the other's boots on the rough board floor. A match scratched and sputtered. Then it was flung down. Running feet padded across the short grass, and Will Arblaster drew up, panting.

"Got it!" he gasped. "The old fool! Put it in a tea canister right on the mantelshelf. Enough to choke a horse! Feel it!"

The lean man, unemotional as ever, reached down and took the roll of money.

"Got another match?" he asked.

Willie struck one, and panting, watched while his companion, moistening a thumb, ruffled through the bills.

"Fifty tens," said the lean man. "Five hundred dollars. Guess I'll carry it."

The bills were **stowed** in a pocket of the belt right next to one of those gold-mounted guns which, earlier in the evening, had covered Willie Arblaster's heart.

"Let's get out of here," the younger urged. Now the hand grasped Will Arblaster's shoulder.

"No, not yet," he said quietly, "not just yet. Get on your horse and set still awhile."

The young man mounted. "What's the idea?"

"Why!" said the level voice at his right. "This is a kind of novelty to me. Robbing trains, you ain't got any chance to see results, like: this here's different. Figure this old guy'll be back pretty soon. I'd like to see what he does when he finds his wad's gone. Ought to be amusing!"

Arblaster chuckled uncertainly.

"Ain't he liable to—"

"He can't see us," said the lean man with a certain new cheerfulness in his tone. "And besides, he'll think we'd naturally be miles away; and besides that, we're mounted already."

"What's that?" whispered the young man, laying a hand on his companion's arm.

The other listened.

"Probably him," he said. "Now stay still."

There were two riders—by their voices, a man and a girl. They were laughing as they approached the rear of the house. They put up the horses. Then their words came clearer to the ears of the listeners, as they turned the corner of the building, walking toward the front door.

"I feel mean about it, anyhow," said the girl's voice. "You going on living here, Daddy, while—"

"Tut-tut-tut!" said the old man. "What's five hundred to me? I ain't never had that much in a lump, and shouldn't know what to do with it if I had. 'Sides, your Aunt Elviry didn't give it to you for nothing. 'If she wants to go to college,' says she, 'let her prove it by workin'. I'll pay half, but she's got to pay t'other half.' Well, you worked, and—Where on earth did I put that key?"

There was a silence, broken by the grunts of the old man as he searched his pockets. Then the girl spoke: the tone of her voice was the more terrible for the restraint she was putting on it.

"Daddy—the—the—did you leave the money in the house?"

"Yes. What is it?" cried the old man.

"Daddy—the door's broken down, and—"

There was a hoarse cry. Boot heels stumbled across the boards. Again a match flared. In one hand Pa Sanderson held the flickering match, in the other a tin box.

"Gone!" he cried in his cracked voice. "Gone!"

Willie Arblaster drew a breath through his teeth and moved uneasily in his saddle. Instantly a lean strong hand, with a grip like steel, fell on his wrist and grasped it. The man behind the hand chuckled.

"Listen!" he said.

"Daddy—Daddy—don't take on so—please don't," came the girl's voice. There was a scrape of chair legs on the floor as she forced the old man into his seat by the fireplace. He hunched there, his face in his hands. She struck a match and laid the flame to the wick of the lamp on the table. As it burned up she went back to her father, knelt by him, and threw her arms about his neck.

"Now, now, now!" she **pleaded.** "Now, Daddy, it's all right. Don't take on so. It's all right."

But he would not be comforted.

"I can't replace it!" cried Pa Sanderson, dropping trembling hands from his face. "It's gone! Two years you've been away from me; two years you've slaved in a store; and now I've—"

"Hush, hush!" the girl begged. "Now, Daddy—it's all right. I can go on working and—"

With an effort, the old man got to his feet. "Two years more slavery, while some skunk drinks your money, gambles it—throws it away!" he cried. "Curse him! Whoever it is, curse him! Where's the justice? What's a man going to believe when years of scraping like your aunt done, and years of slaving like yours in Laredo there, and all our happiness today can be wiped out by a thief in a minute?"

The girl put her little hand over her father's mouth.

"Don't, Daddy," she choked. "It only makes it worse. Come and lie down on your bed, and I'll make you some coffee. Don't cry, Daddy. Please."

Gently she led the old man out of the circle of lamplight. The listeners could hear the sounds of weeping.

The lean man sniffed, chuckled, and pulled his bridle.

"Some circus!" he said appreciatively. "C'mon, boy."

His horse moved a few paces, but Will Arblaster's did not. The lean man turned in his saddle.

"Ain't you coming?" he asked.

For ten seconds, perhaps, the boy made no answer. Then he urged his pony forward until it stood side by side with his companion's.

"No," he said. "And—and I ain't going to take that money, neither."

"Huh?"

The voice was slow and meditative.

"Don't know as ever I figured what this game meant," he said. "Always seemed to me that all the hardships was on the stick-up man's side—getting shot at and chased and so on. Kind of fun, at that. Never thought about—old men crying."

"That ain't my fault," said the lean man.

"No," said Will Arblaster, still very slowly. "But I'm going to take that money back. You didn't have no trouble getting it, so you don't lose nothing."

"Suppose I say I won't let go of it?" suggested the lean man with a sneer.

"Then," snarled Arblaster, "I'll blow your head off and take it! Don't you move, you! I've got you covered. I'll take the money out myself."

His revolver muzzle under his companion's nose, he snapped open the pocket of the belt and took out the roll of bills. Then he swung off his horse and shambled into the lighted doorway of the cabin. The lean man sat perfectly still.

It was a full ten minutes before Will Arblaster came back alone. He stumbled forward through the darkness toward his horse. Still the lean man did not move.

"I'm—sorry," said the boy as he mounted. "But—"

"I ain't," said the lean man quietly. "What do you think I made you stay and watch for, you young fool?"

The boy made no reply. Suddenly the hair prickled on the back of his neck and his jaw fell.

"Say," he demanded hoarsely at last. "Ain't you Pecos Tommy?"

The lean man's answer was a short laugh.

"But you got his guns, and the people in Longhorn all kind of fell back!" the boy cried. "If you ain't him, who are you?"

The moon had drifted from behind a cloud. It flung a ray of light across the face of the lean man as he turned it, narrow-eyed, toward Arblaster.

"Why," said the lean man dryly, "I'm the sheriff that killed him yesterday. Let's be riding back."

GETTING THE MEANING OF THE STORY.
Complete each of the following sentences
by putting an *x* in the box next to the
correct answer. Each sentence helps you
get the meaning of the story.

1. Will Arblaster thought that the lean
   man was Pecos Tommy because the man
   - [ ] a. looked like Pecos Tommy.
   - [ ] b. said he was Pecos Tommy.
   - [x] c. was wearing Pecos Tommy's
         gold-mounted guns.

2. Will Arblaster knew that Pa Sanderson
   had a roll of cash because
   - [x] a. Will saw him come out of the
         bank with it.
   - [ ] b. Pa Sanderson always carried a
         lot of money with him.
   - [ ] c. Will heard that Sanderson was
         planning to give his daughter
         the cash.

3. After Will took the money, the lean
   man insisted that they
   - [ ] a. get away from there quickly.
   - [x] b. stay and watch to see what would
         happen.
   - [ ] c. think of how to spend the cash.

4. At the end of the story, Will decided to
   - [x] a. give the money back.
   - [ ] b. join Pecos Tommy's gang.
   - [ ] c. force the lean man to turn
         himself in.

REVIEWING STORY ELEMENTS. Each of
the following questions reviews your
understanding of story elements. Put an
x in the box next to the correct answer
to each question.

1. What happened last in the *plot* of
   the story?
   - [x] a. The lean man announced that
         he was the sheriff.
   - [ ] b. Pa Sanderson realized that the
         money was gone.
   - [ ] c. Will Arblaster broke into the cabin.

2. Which sentence best *characterizes* Will
   Arblaster?
   - [ ] a. He found life exciting and was
         happy with his job.
   - [ ] b. He was afraid of being caught.
   - [x] c. He was not as cruel and heartless
         as he thought he was.

3. What is the *setting* of "Gold-Mounted
   Guns"?
   - [ ] a. a city in the East
   - [ ] b. a farm in the South
   - [x] c. the Old West

4. Pick the sentence which best tells the
   theme of the story.
   - [x] a. When a young man sees the pain
         he has caused others, he learns
         a lesson.
   - [ ] b. A young woman cannot afford
         to go to school when her money
         is stolen.
   - [ ] c. People cannot really change.

[___] × 5 = [___]

NUMBER   YOUR
CORRECT   SCORE

[___] × 5 = [___]

NUMBER   YOUR
CORRECT   SCORE

EXAMINING VOCABULARY WORDS. Answer the following vocabulary questions by putting an *x* in the box next to the correct answer. The vocabulary words are printed in **boldface** in the story. If you wish, look back at the words before you answer the questions.

1. The lean man stowed the cash in a pocket of the belt. What is the meaning of the word *stowed?*
   ☒ a. packed
   ☐ b. lost
   ☐ c. opened

2. There was the heavy thud of a shoulder against wood—and a crash as the door went down. What is a *thud?*
   ☐ a. a scream
   ☒ b. a dull sound
   ☐ c. a marching band

3. Will Arblaster gave the lean man the details of the job he had planned. Which of the following best defines the word *details?*
   ☐ a. rewards or prizes
   ☐ b. best answers
   ☒ c. small pieces of information

4. "Daddy, it's all right. Don't take on so," the young woman pleaded. The word *pleaded* means
   ☒ a. urged strongly.
   ☐ b. wondered about.
   ☐ c. worked hard.

	× 5 =	
NUMBER CORRECT		YOUR SCORE

ADDING WORDS TO A PASSAGE. Complete the following paragraph by filling in each blank with one of the words listed in the box below. Each of the words appears in the story. Since there are five words and four blanks, one word in the group will not be used.

Life in the Old West was sometimes dangerous. Outlaws often decided to _*join*_ together in gangs. These gangs robbed _*trains*_ and held up banks. There were few sheriffs and fewer jails. Often a _*sheriff*_ had to keep order in an area hundreds of miles in size. It was difficult, but after a _*while*_ , law was finally brought to the Old West.

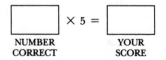

hill	join
sheriff	
while	trains

	× 5 =	
NUMBER CORRECT		YOUR SCORE

THINKING ABOUT THE STORY. Each of the following questions will help you to think critically about the selection. Put an *x* in the box next to the correct answer.

1. What would have happened if Will Arblaster had decided to ride off with the cash?
   ☐ a. He would have escaped.
   ☐ b. He would have become the lean man's partner.
   ☒ c. He would have been arrested by the sheriff.

2. Why did the lean man make Will stay and watch?
   ☒ a. He wanted Will to see the sadness and suffering he caused.
   ☐ b. He thought that Will would think the scene was funny.
   ☐ c. The lean man had no place to go and was not in a hurry to leave.

3. How did Will feel when he saw what happened because he stole the cash?
   ☒ a. He was very sorry.
   ☐ b. He was pleased.
   ☐ c. He didn't care.

4. How did the Sandersons probably feel after Will Arblaster left them?
   ☐ a. angry for being so careless
   ☒ b. amazed and delighted
   ☐ c. afraid that he would return

Thinking More about the Story. Your teacher might want you to write your answers.

• At the beginning of the story, Will Arblaster thought that the lean man was Pecos Tommy. Why didn't the lean man tell Will that he was the sheriff then?
• Will asked the lean man, "If I do the job right, will you take me along?" The lean man answered: "Yeah—I'll take you along." What did he *really* mean by this answer? Explain.
• His experience with the sheriff changed Will's life forever. Do you agree with this statement? Give reasons to support your answer.

Use the boxes below to total your scores for the exercises.

	GETTING THE MEANING OF THE STORY
+	
	REVIEWING STORY ELEMENTS
+	
	EXAMINING VOCABULARY WORDS
+	
	ADDING WORDS TO A PASSAGE
+	
	THINKING ABOUT THE STORY
▼	
	Score Total: Story 15

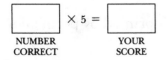

☐ × 5 = ☐

NUMBER   YOUR
CORRECT   SCORE

Acknowledgments

Acknowledgment is gratefully made to the following publishers, authors, and agents for permission to reprint these works. Adaptations are by Burton Goodman.

"A Secret for Two" by Quentin Reynolds. © 1936, Crowell-Collier Publishing Company. Reprinted by permission of the Estate of Quentin Reynolds.

"The Romance of a Busy Broker" by O. Henry. Reprinted by permission of Doubleday, a division of Bantam, Doubleday, Dell Publishing Group, Inc.

"Mrs. Packletide's Tiger" by Saki. Reprinted by permission of Viking Penguin, Inc.

"The Piping-Hot Pizza Mystery" by Elizabeth VanSteenwyk. Reprinted by permission of Elizabeth VanSteenwyk.

"The Gift of the Magi" by O. Henry. Reprinted by permission of Doubleday, a division of Bantam, Doubleday, Dell Publishing Group, Inc.

"The Southpaw" by Judith Viorst. © 1974 by Judith Viorst. From *Free To Be . . . You and Me.*

"His Father's Boots" by Charles Land. Reprinted by permission of Larry Sternig Literary Agency.

"The Angel" by Carol Chapman. Reprinted by permission of Carol Chapman.

"Pop's Boy" by Irvin Ashkenazy. All efforts were made to locate the copyright holder, but no clear record exists with Twayne Publishers.

"Ooka and the Stolen Smell" by I. G. Edmonds. Reprinted by permission of

Progress Chart

1. Write in your score for each exercise.
2. Write in your Total Score.

	G	R	E	A	T	TOTAL SCORE
Story 1						
Story 2						
Story 3						
Story 4						
Story 5						
Story 6						
Story 7						
Story 8						
Story 9						
Story 10						
Story 11						
Story 12						
Story 13						
Story 14						
Story 15						

Progress Graph

1. Write your Total Score in the box under the number for each story.
2. Put an *x* along the line above each box to show your Total Score for that story.
3. Make a graph of your progress by drawing a line to connect the *x*'s.

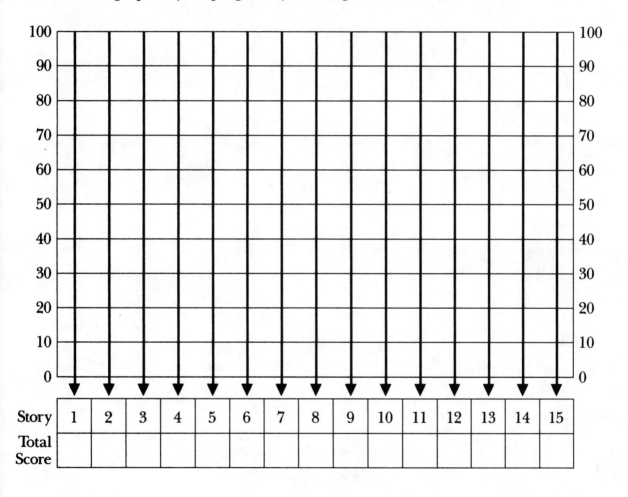

Story	1	2	3	4	5	6	7	8	9	10	11	12	13	14	15
Total Score															

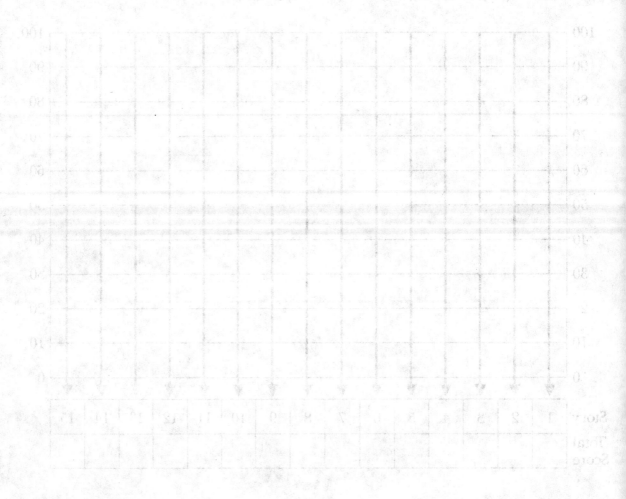